CON

Dedicated to the memory of Doreen Valiente.

Acknowledgements
I am very grateful to Jane Brideson for her help with this book.
Jane's training schedule has formed the basis for the chapter
layouts, but even more valuable has been the fact that she has
always been there to discuss, refine and clarify ideas. Several of
Jane's own ideas have been incorporated into my approach,
resulting in a clearer and more helpful book. Thank you, Jane.

I also acknowledge the indirect help of several writers in clarifying
my ideas. No doubt I have drawn on them more than I realise,
because their words of wisdom have become a part of me. They are:
Starhawk, Doreen Valiente, Shan, Marian Green, Janet and Stewart
Farrar, Rae Beth, Vivianne Crowley and no doubt others whom I
cannot bring to mind. Thank you all for your gifts of the craft.

Order queries: please contact Bookpoint Ltd, 130 Milton Park,
Abingdon, Oxon OX14 4SB. Telephone: (44) 01235 400414,
Fax: (44) 01235 400454. Lines are open from 9.00–6.00, Monday to
Saturday, with a 24-hour message answering service.
Email address: orders@bookpoint.co.uk

British Library Cataloguing in Publication Data
A catalogue record for this title is available from The British Library

ISBN 0 340 753242

First published 2000
Impression number   10 9 8 7 6 5 4 3
Year   2005 2004 2003 2002 2001

Copyright © 2000 Teresa Moorey

Typeset by Transet Limited, Coventry, England.
Printed in Great Britain for Hodder & Stoughton Educational, a division
of Hodder Headline plc, 338 Euston Road, London NW1 3BH by
Cox & Wyman Ltd, Reading, Berkshire.

INTRODUCTION

Witchcraft isn't easy to introduce, for the Craft can never be dissected, nor finally defined. It's about our essence, and what we may become. It's about doing, feeling, wayfaring, being. We can look for signposts to direct us or offer alternative pathways. This book is a set of signposts, but it is not a description of the journey, because that journey is yours, and it is a mystery.

Down the tunnels of time echo the whispers of the Craft of the Wise. From the mute meditations of the stones and the chant of the wind in the trees, through people who danced and murmured the story into the dawn of consciousness, this ancient knowingness has taken shape. From the time of the grandmothers, through centuries of conquest and domination, through bad times and burning times, the craft has endured. Now it is resurrecting, bringing the old knowledge of hill and forest, stone and bone into a modern context, fit for the dawning of a new era.

Witchcraft is a spiritual and magical system, and a way to personal growth. It has no dogma, for it encourages personal revelation and responsibility. Valuing the instinctual, the mystical and the power of the individual, because it identifies with Nature and the Goddess, witchcraft has often been denigrated and persecuted by a mistrustful culture that devalues the Feminine. However, witches are certainly coming out of the broom cupboard. Dusty canons may crumble, but witchcraft is identified as having relevance and a vital message in the world of the twenty-first century. Reanimating our sense of Nature seems a survival necessity, while developing our connection to the

Divine is now, for many people, the only sort of spirituality that can be trusted.

There are many forms of witchcraft, in a sense as many as there are individual witches. This book is as general an overview as possible, giving as many different pointers as I can. But witchcraft can't be explained. Rather it needs to be discovered. Essentially it has always been a practical matter, and from grove to cottage kitchen its main aim was and is to get results. Witchcraft, as so many similar traditions, was originally oral, and while the Craft here described is essentially born of European consciousness, below the surface it shares much with others, for instance the Native Americans. Indeed it is probable that we all share a common origin.

You may want to use this book as a training manual, and I have made every effort to give as thorough a grounding as possible in the Training Sessions. Witchcraft isn't just about reading and thinking, but about feeling, experiencing, doing and creating. However, if you just want to find out about witchcraft, this should help you understand and be well informed. But remember, these are only my words, on a subject too deep to be contained in any words. I offer pointers, and if you follow with your heart you will discover much more than I could ever describe.

Teresa Moorey, Samhain, 1999

1

WITCHCRAFT, ROOT
AND BRANCH

*Behold, I have been with thee from the beginning,
and I am that which is attained at the end of desire.*

DOREEN VALIENTE, *THE CHARGE OF THE GODDESS*

WHAT IS WITCHCRAFT?

So simple a question, and yet so difficult. We may not ask ourselves exactly what witchcraft is until our feet are well down the path, because we have been following our own spiritual beacon. Or we may not ask it at all until someone else says, 'What exactly are you, then?' At this moment we realize we have no words for the mysteries or the truth, that beckon in the moonlight or shine in the sunlit meadow. Witchcraft is not really a product of the intellect, rising as it does from the shadows of our consciousness, but struggling for the apt phrase to define it can be a great help in organizing our own concepts. In the end this can aid us on our paths as witches, because it helps to prevent our logical minds from tripping us up. It also helps foster a general understanding of witchcraft, for while the Craft is far from evangelical, it may be seen as the responsibility of each witch to give as good an account of the path as she or he is able, to give greater freedom of choice to others. In this sense, every witch is a priestess or priest.

The best way to define witchcraft is to describe it as a form of Nature and Goddess worship, with all that that entails.

What it entails, of course, is a very great deal, for the Craft does not transfer monotheistic systems and attitudes to reverence for Nature, and the Goddess is not 'God in drag'! Worship of the Goddess is radically different from worship of the Fathergod, because it encourages personal revelation and the pursuance of an individual path, without dogma or hierarchy. Nature is the gospel of the witches: our litany is the wind in the grass. 'Thou shalt nots' are brushed away by the Great Mother, who encourages enjoyment of the world and the senses as an act of Her worship. Witchcraft encourages a sense of immanence, the feeling that deity is within the natural world, infusing it with vibrancy and beauty, and fostering the development of personal power and effectuality. Added to an emphasis on the instinctual and non-rational, this means the working of magic. So there are three main aspects to witchcraft: personal growth, the spiritual path and the magical system. These are all encapsulated and implied in 'Goddess worship'.

Not that worship of the God is not a vital part of witchcraft, because most witches do honour Him for Himself and also as consort to the Goddess. He is referred to as 'the God' rather than 'God' because He is not monolithic and singular, as in patriarchal religions. Theoretically it might be possible to be a witch and worship a single, masculine deity, but it is hard to imagine the spirit of witchcraft remaining intact in this atmosphere. The witches' God is playful, with as much testosterone as a rutting stag! He is not punitive or judgemental. Rather He is wild and wise, strong, gentle and protective. Goddess and God will be fully explored in the next chapter.

Because witchcraft is such a fluid system, no definition can satisfy fully. Witches come in all shapes and sizes, and are of many different persuasions. There are witches who worship Jesus, and there are witches who follow the spirit of Nature, without the person of Goddess or God. In the end, what

unites witches is a feeling, an approach, an ambience.
Witches are vividly aware of the power underlying the
manifest world, connecting it, animating it. Instinctively
they work with this power, mystics and pragmatists,
gleefully sensual, yet with their eyes focused on Otherworld.

THE HISTORY OF THE CRAFT

There is no exact and verified history of witchcraft, and
there are many reasons for this. In the first place, it is in the
very nature of witchcraft to be mysterious – it is, after all, a
'mystery cult'. Until fairly recently, witches did not like
information about their art to be generally available, and
today every witch and group of witches will have secrets.
Moreover, some things can only be discovered by
experience. Secondly, witchcraft, and similar traditions,
have been passed down by word of mouth from we-know-
not-when, often by people who were essentially simple.
This can make for something as inscrutable as it is distorted.
Last but not least, witches have been persecuted horribly
throughout history. Any medieval witch would have
practised in the utmost secrecy, under constant fear of
torture and a ghastly death. In England, the law against
witchcraft was repealed in 1951, at the behest of Winston
Churchill, who perceived it had been used in a repressive
and archaic form (describing it as 'obsolete tomfoolery')
against the materialization medium, Helen Duncan. Since
then the climate has become progressively more free, with
the last decade seeing an immense growth in the popularity
of witchcraft and paganism in general, and increased
dialogue between pagans, Christians and others. However,
let us go back to the beginning ...

Over the long and misty centuries of the Palaeolithic era,
enshrined in grey stone, the Great Mother reigned

unchallenged. She was the source of life, and to Her all returned at death. The tomb was also Her womb, to bring forth new life as the seasons turned. In Her lay the mystery of the Unmanifest and the Manifest. The female of the tribe, bringing forth life from their own bodies, mediated with the Goddess for men, and society was matriarchal, or at least matrifocal, which means that if women were not exactly the head of a hierarchy, the working, social and ritual aspects of life orbited around influential women. This is the picture painted by many historians, and while there is not universal agreement, the indications are that female power was greater in prehistory. Goddess figures from more than 20,000 years ago have been unearthed, showing the generous figure of the Creatrix. One of the most well known is that of the 'Venus of Willendorf' in Austria, made of limestone and standing 11 cms (4^1/$_2$ in) tall. Similar male figures have not been found. The image of the caveman dragging his mate away by her hair is patriarchal wishful thinking!

Some scholars have gone even further back. The writer Stan Gooch in *Cities of Dreams: When Women Ruled the Earth* (see Further Reading) puts forward the notion that Neanderthal man lived in a flourishing civilization, largely nocturnal and Moon-worshipping and driven by women, sex and magic. Neanderthal man had a large cerebellum, the 'bun' at the back of the head that houses the part of the brain associated with psychic powers, and there is evidence that he was culturally advanced and highly intelligent. Gooch states that Cro-Magnon man did not wipe out Neanderthal man, but conquered and interbred with them, for they feared the Neanderthal magic, they wanted it for themselves. Many of the characteristics Gooch attributes to the Neanderthals are decidedly 'witchy' and many have since been the subject of persecution and fear, such as left-handedness, use of the number 13 (also related to the motions of the Moon), dark or red hair, nocturnal activities, psychism, preoccupation with the Feminine, including menstruation. If this is true, our lineage may be more ancient than any witch could wish!

Some have seen the ancient Great Mother as androgyne, embodying aspects of the masculine within Her. However, as the male aspect of procreation came to be appreciated, the persona of the God took His defined place alongside the Goddess. Not only were humans part of the continuum of creation, they also intentionally ruptured it by the killing of creatures in the hunt. So alongside the all-embracing story of the Mother, rituals also arose for he who must violate the oneness. Here may have been one origin of the God. Living creatures were seen as emanating from the Great Mother, and the God arose in the life force of animals. This evolved into the God as son/lover to the Goddess, born, growing, mating, dying and born again, while the Goddess remained constant. With the progress of agriculture the God was also the Corn Spirit, cut down each Autumn, to rise again the following Spring. No doubt magic was practised to ensure success in the hunt and the field. This was probably 'sympathetic magic' done on the 'like attracts like' principle. For instance, wearing antlers and doing a stag-dance would connect the hunter to the spirit of the deer that he was going to pursue the following day. Forming a 'dolly' from the ripened corn (a practice that has survived to this day) keeps alive the spirit within the corn, to be revived the following Spring.

As the Bronze Age gave way to the Iron Age, war and destruction came upon what was essentially a peaceful European culture. Fire, the sword and masculine strength took the place of female rhythms. Hierarchy, fear and might-is-right overtook the agrarian dream time. However, while this must have been a time of darkness and horror, it was also a time of development for individual ego-consciousness and the logical, scientific and competitive approach that has given us so many of our modern comforts (as well as pollution, weapons of mass destruction and many other evils we know so well). Feminine power went into abeyance, although there is evidence to suggest that women still held considerable power in Celtic society, and much of contemporary witchcraft is Celtic in origin. The Celts were a cultural rather than a racial grouping who had become a major force in Europe by 500 BCE (CE and BCE stand for Common Era and Before Common Era, terms preferred by pagans). The Celts have passed down to us the four major seasonal festivals of Beltane, Lughnasadh, Samhain and Imbolc, which were significant in the lives of herding peoples. The Great Mother was worshipped by the matrifocal Celts, along with a wide array of goddesses and gods, and the calendar depended on the Moon. However, it is the Celtic attitude, that sense of Otherworld, of twists and turns, tricks and hidden meanings, as well as some inspiring and subtle manifestations of goddesses and gods, that form possibly their most notable legacy to modern witchcraft.

While some witches are expressly Celtic in the forms of Goddess and God they honour, and in their practices, modern witchcraft is influenced by two strands of thought from the continent, which can be called the Apollonian and Dionysian. In his classic work *The White Goddess* (see Further Reading) Robert Graves identified two types of 'knowledge': 'solar' knowledge and 'lunar' knowledge. The former is a product of the conscious mind, while the latter concerns the instincts and psychic faculties. These are generally associated with left brain and right brain respectively. Apollo came to be known as the Sun god, and his cult was concerned with philosophy, reflection and the 'light' of consciousness. Dionysus was the god of wine and ecstasy. Not for him the stately measure in the temple sanctum, but a divine madness in Nature's secret spots. Both of these approaches sought to raise the consciousness of the participants, and both are discernible in contemporary witchcraft: the Apollonian element is present in the construction of rituals, while the ambience, the states of trance and the spontaneity of actions are Dionysian in essence.

The cult of Egyptian Isis has also been influential. As a goddess, her form was complete, and her influence widespread. In the way characteristic of Goddess worship, inner revelation was fostered in the devotee, and this lingered in the early Christian cult of Gnosticism (*gnosis* means knowing, and the belief emphasized a direct inner experience of God). It then reappeared in the Cathar heresy in southern France, which was stamped out by the Church in the Middle Ages in a campaign of unparalleled ferocity. In the Gnostic gospels the Feminine is worshipped as 'Sophia, first begetress and Mother of the Universe', and in the Gnostic Church women held rank, taught and prophesied. Gnosticism was suppressed in the fourth century CE by Constantine, the first Christian emperor, who, incidentally, boiled his wife alive and slew his son! However, Gnosticism remained alive and well in the study of alchemy and magic in the Middle Ages, and has resurfaced again today in a variety of forms, witchcraft being one example.

Historically much closer, and allied to the cult of Isis, were the Eleusinian mysteries in classical Greece. The myth of Persephone/Kore, who is abducted by the underworld god, Pluto, while her mother Demeter, goddess of Nature, is left to mourn, is another embodiment of the natural cycles and the mystery of life-in-death, death-in-life, carried by the Goddess, and explored by the Eleusinian initiates. Over the temple door at Eleusis were inscribed the words, 'Know thyself', a phrase that holds great resonance for witches today. An echo of the Eleusinian ceremonies lingers in present-day Autumn Equinox rites, when witches contemplate an ear of wheat with the words, 'In silence is the seed of wisdom gained'. In Eleusis, the mysteries were celebrated for almost 2,000 years until they were forbidden by the Christian philosopher Theophrastus. Later the ancient temples were sacked by the Goths.

The old gods were companionable. A traveller from a foreign land might recognize his beloved Rhiannon as Epona, or might find Lugh Longhand in Apollo. Wars there were a plenty, but pagan faiths blended comfortably. Witch-burning was not a Christian invention, for the Greek Demosthenes (384–322 BCE) recounts how a witch was tried and burnt in Athens. However, while most monarchs were wary of those who might undermine the state through magic, for the most part it was accepted in wise women, cunning men, priests and priestesses who mediated the Divine through their presence. Christianity changed most of that, with its message of one crystalline and literal truth, one judgemental and masculine God, and the belief that saviour from eternal damnation was achievable not through an inward quest but through the mediation of an ordained priesthood – all of whom were men. Mysticism, transcendence, direct experience of the Divine were not relevant: obedience to dogma was. The new faith was based less upon the loving teachings of Jesus and more on the preachings of St Paul, who hated women. Naturally this religion was and is profoundly uneasy about witches, who embody all that is feminine and instinctual. Initially the position of the Church was that witches were simply deluded Goddess worshippers, as set out in the *Canon Episcopi,* published in the early tenth century. However, this was not enough to root out all of the dissidents, so teachings were altered to portray witches as evil worshippers of Satan, bringers of trouble and misfortune – an ironical attitude in view of the fact that witchcraft does not polarize 'good' and 'evil', and certainly holds no belief in the Devil, or similar. This approach was embodied in the notorious *Malleus Maleficarum,* a handbook for witch-hunters, translated by Montagu Summers and published in 1486, in which witches are credited with all manner of abominations.

Accounts of the witch hunts of the Middle Ages recall a time of stark terror and savage cruelty, as neighbour denounced neighbour to the witch-finders. Subjects were tortured without mercy and when they 'confessed', they were burnt, most often alive, although in England (as opposed to in the rest of the British Isles), witches were hanged instead. However, heresy meant death by burning, and so, before the Reformation, English witches could be burnt. Treason backed up by witchcraft was a burnable offence, and to kill one's husband was a crime known as 'petty treason'. As late as 1776 a Mrs Cruttenden was publicly burnt in Horsham, England, for allegedly cutting her husband's throat. The persecutors of witches enacted horrors far worse than any crime of the wretched accused, and it is hard to understand how this madness could have held sway for so long throughout Europe. Simple paranoia lay at its root, that comfortable process of projecting all our own shortcomings onto someone else and deciding to hate them, instead of reforming ourselves. Those who feared the vengeance of Fathergod on their natural lusts no doubt felt safer if there were witches to be rooted our for the attention of the Almighty! Some say as many as nine million people died in this way during the Middle Ages and the majority of them were women, from the poorer classes, although this figure is disputed.

The practice of magic did not die out, however. It continued in more Apollonian form, with ritual magicians, usually men from the better classes, ostentatiously invoking saints and prophets for their endeavours. Meanwhile, old and primitive Nature magic is believed to have survived in rural areas of Europe. However, most historical accounts are unclear. 'Real' witches would have kept pretty quiet, and most information extracted under torture can hardly be considered reliable. In addition, most of the unfortunate victims were not witches, by any definition, and some historians even assert that there was virtually no 'real' witchcraft in the Middle Ages.

Although intent on stamping out the old religion, the Church in fact incorporated as many of the old beliefs and customs as possible into its own observances. Thus Samhain became All Hallows E'en, and Yule became Christmas. By express order of Pope Gregory I in 601 CE, churches were constructed on old sites sacred to pagan faiths (although

The Sheil-na-Gig and the Green Man provide clues of ancient beliefs and practices

some historians now dispute that this took place), and many old churches still display pagan carvings, such as the Green Man, and Sheila-na-gig. It has also been asserted that many English monarchs were members of a witch cult, especially the Plantagenets, whose name derives from the broom plant, *planta genista,* which was used in the making of the besom, the broom on which witches were believed to fly. The well-known story of 'the Fair Maid of Kent' is a case in point. Her garter fell to the floor while she was dancing and was restored to her, gallantly, by King Edward III (1312–77) with the immortal words, 'Honi soit qui mal y pense. Garters were a hallmark of witches of rank and by his words, which roughly translate as, 'Evil be to him that evil thinks', Edward issued a cryptic challenge to those assembled. He subsequently founded the Order of the Garter, Britain's premier chivalric order, with twelve knights for himself and twelve for his son, who was interestingly called The Black Prince. This meant there were two groups of thirteen – a witchy number, also allied to the Moon, as the moon makes 13 yearly cycles.

There are several other examples of royalty and witchcraft, for instance, the mysterious meeting of Elizabeth Woodville and Edward IV (1442–83) in eerie Whittlewood Forest, their marriage on May Day, and Elizabeth's later accusation of witchcraft. The White Boar (a pagan symbol) on the flag of Richard III (1452–85) had the crescent-shaped tusks associated with the Moon. Richard, as last of the Plantagenets, was maligned by the incoming Tudors, and misrepresented by Shakespeare, with much accusation and counter-accusation occurring behind the scenes. An earlier example of witchy kings is that of William II also known as William Rufus (1056–1100), who died, along with the Corn King, at the feast of Lammas in 1100 CE in the New Forest. Rufus was openly pagan, and seemed to embrace willingly the traditional ritual death of more ancient monarchs, in honour of the dying God.

As the Age of Reason fostered a degree of detachment, witches were less feared and, in the light of scientific advancement, the existence of magic was rejected as superstition. Paradoxically, this more clement climate gradually fostered a witchcraft revival. As the nineteenth century unfolded, interest in the occult, spiritualism and the afterlife gained momentum. At the turn of the century, the traveller and writer Charles Leland produced a work called *Aradia, or Gospel of the Witches* (see Further Reading) about the ancient Craft in Tuscany, Italy. Although its mythology is mixed, and some of its rites tinged with the malevolence of a repressed peasantry, this work forms the basis of some modern rituals. Early in the twentieth century, Margaret Murray, anthropologist and Egyptologist, produced *The Witch Cult in Western Europe*, *The God of the Witches* and *The Divine King in England* (see Further Reading), describing an extensive system of witchcraft in which the English monarchy were active. However, the principle exponent of contemporary witchcraft was Gerald Gardner, who was initiated into a coven in the New Forest, and offended many by publicizing their rituals, with many embellishments of his own! Some of his contemporaries were even less than pleased at the repeal of the witchcraft laws in 1951, believing that this would lay the Craft open to penetration by those whose motives were questionable. However, Gardner is now regarded with general respect and, despite his possible shortcomings, was a great exponent of the Craft, a man of immense personal influence and charm, and essentially the founder of modern Wicca.

In his exploration of ancient myths in *The White Goddess*, Robert Graves has earnt a place in the witchcraft Hall of Fame, although there are those who consider him to be spurious, to some degree. Aleister Crowley, the infamous 'Great Beast', is another twentieth-century figure who had some influence on present-day thought and understanding of the occult. He was not a witch, and displayed a distrust of women, but his evil reputation is unjustified. He had links with an East Anglian cunning man called George Pickingill, as also did Gerald Gardner. Crowley is notable for his irrepressible and public pursuance of the occult and magic. Last but not least in our list of recent figures comes Alex Sanders, founder of Alexandrian Wicca, said by some to have been initiated into a Gardnerian coven, and by others to have been initiated into a traditional path by his grandmother.

In the latter part of this century, witchcraft has developed, becoming a subject for open debate, with many different paths open to the seeker. Of course, paranoia has not disappeared, and there are still those who confuse witchcraft with Satanism. On the night of 20 March 1990, in Dillsburg PA in America, police arrested seven teenagers who were heavily armed with guns and explosives. They claimed to be 'Christian solders' who had heard that

Satanists emerged at the Equinox, and were going to hunt down and 'deal with' any woodland worshippers. Despite such incidents, interfaith dialogue grows between pagans and monotheistic faiths, and witchcraft emerges ever more clearly as an inspiring spiritual path with a valuable message as we go into the new millennium.

WHY THE 'W' WORD?

As we know that the Craft is about worship of Nature and the Goddess, and a path to the Divine, why do we continue to use a word that is inextricably linked, in history and fairy story, to the evil and destructive? Someone recently said to me, 'It's a pity it's called by that word. It's frightening'.

I think witches cling to the 'W' word for many reasons. Firstly, there is plenty of the rebel in most witches, and they don't see why they should sell out to those who are prejudiced. It is argued that 'Witch' has the same root as 'wise', and many witches feel that the true meaning of the word has been twisted to become something nasty. Secondly, now that we are free to come out of the broom-cupboard, it seems disloyal to renege on a word in the name of which so many of our sisters and brothers have died. Finally, there is a delicious, shivery feel to the word 'witch', and this holds more than a hint of the paradox of the path itself. While witches work only for positive things, they explicitly honour the powers of darkness and destruction, not as inimical to creation, but as part of it, as anabolism and catabolism are both necessary parts of metabolism, and as Winter and Summer both have a place in the seasonal spectrum. This view even finds expression in the Bible in Isiah 45:7, 'I form the light and create darkness. I make peace and create evil. I the Lord do all these things'. Witches are proud that they are not afraid of their own shadow.

CONTEMPORARY PATHS

No one can make you a witch, for it is something that you alone decide and affirm. Nor is a witch something you become, rather it is something you are, and you discover this, and develop it. A witch is a witch, is a witch. You can train yourself, you can become one on your own, and you can be one on your own, without the need for anyone else to initiate you, or to admit you into an occult hierarchy. Indeed, it is only in the secret depths of the heart that the witch-fire is kindled. Having said this, there are many advantages to training with and drawing from the experience of a group of people, and even those who do not seem very wise can have a great deal to offer. Whichever path you choose, it is vital to study, practise and achieve a thorough grounding, and this can be easier if someone else is training you. However, in the end, you must take responsibility for your own development. Witchcraft certainly isn't intellectual, although some people approach it in this way. It is beautiful and natural, but you will have to do some hard work along the way. I am sure you will enjoy it.

Perhaps the most well-defined form of witchcraft is Wicca. As we have seen, Wicca as it is practised today was developed by Gerald Gardner and Alex Sanders. Wiccan covens have a hierarchy of initiations, starting with the beginner, or neophyte, and then progressing to first, second and third degrees. The final degree confirms the Wiccan as a potential High Priestess or Priest, able to form their own coven. Covens can comprise any reasonable number of witches (usually between three and fifteen), and do not have to be evenly composed of masculine and feminine – which is just as well, as fewer men are drawn to the Craft than women! However, there will always be at least one male present – in the person of the High Priest – and the majority of covens are headed by a High Priest and Priestess who are live-in partners, if not a conventionally married couple. The High Priestess is the coven leader, but she is 'first among equals' rather than superior.

Part of the Wiccan training includes the copying out of the Book of Shadows, which describes rituals for the Craft. Some say that the Book is derived from very ancient material, although, given that most people in the Middle Ages couldn't write, this is doubtful. There is more than a hint of the Victorian in the poetic ring of the invocations, and some of the rituals are allied to the Jewish magical system of the Qabalah. Wiccans celebrate eight annual festivals in rituals that are prescribed, although there is room for some spontaneity, usually after the more formal business has been completed. Specific magic may also be worked, as well as seasonal observance. Coven members are expected to be discrete about the identity of others, if this is called for. Wiccan rituals are usually conducted 'sky-clad', which means nude, and this makes for a very special, intimate and powerful atmosphere. Sexual exploitation is utterly prohibited and no one under the age of eighteen is admitted. Lots of stress is laid upon feasting after the rituals, and this is great fun!

The advantages to Wicca are that it is quite formal with clear rituals and practices, making it easy to participate in at any level. By the same token, those who prefer more spontaneity may regard this as a disadvantage. There may be a feeling of achievement in going up the ladder of initiations, and Wicca is a tried-and-tested system with some experienced practitioners. However, non-Wiccans feel that it is too authoritarian and even old-fashioned. They believe the hierarchy smacks of patriarchy and is just a little too dogmatic in places (some Wiccans have been heard to assert that male/female polarity is essential in the workings of magic and even that homosexuality is suspect). The chief drawback to Wicca seems to be allied to the hierarchy, which has little to do with one's ability as a witch (whatever that may be) – indeed, the Third Degree may be acquired by anyone who has a reasonable memory and deportment, and spends enough time in the Craft. On the other hand, it could be that its relative solidity and structure have done much for the acceptance of the Craft.

Other forms of the Craft are less well defined, but nonetheless attract followers in growing numbers. One path is that of the Hedge-witch, who usually works alone, or sometimes with a partner, joining a group for some of the festivals. I believe that the term 'Hedge-witch' derives from the Celtic reverence for boundaries as magical crossover points, and that the Hedge-witch is a dweller of the fringes of society, and of the edges of Otherworld. It is possibly the most mystical of paths. It can be very lonely, and there isn't always anyone to talk things through with, so mistakes can be made. Much effort is required to set up rituals on one's own, and this may be less fun. However, it may be the path to a vivid inner experience.

Traditional groups exist, whose rituals are based on ancient practice, and there are many variations on these rituals. In the end, I do not believe that anyone can feel sure that their way is totally 'traditional' because there must always be loss, gain and change as knowledge and practice is passed on. Each group must be assessed on its own methods. Most groups' practices seem to be less formal than Wicca, and contemporary groups evolve naturally, with people getting together and making their own rituals and celebrations. A more open style is also developing, with public festivals and eco-magic. There is mostly a strongly feminine influence, but the Craft is equally attractive to men who wish to discover their more sensitive, intuitive side, and many feel that it enhances their masculinity, giving them joy in the strength of their drives, and enabling them to find greater inner peace and balance. Heterosexual men seek to honour the Feminine and find their gentler side, and gay men often find much in the Craft to inspire (homosexuals and witches have been subject to similar persecution through history). The general emphasis is always on personal development, shamanism, the mantic arts, healing, traditional crafts and environmental concerns. It is not unusual for witches to come from varied backgrounds and to work in a variety of ways, sometimes alone, sometimes in a group or a couple, sometimes esoterically in rituals that work on the inner planes, and sometimes exoterically, in the outside world, with customs involving family and friends. Witchcraft certainly has a political aspect, and while this book concentrates on the esoteric, any witch who is truly a witch will not confine the Craft solely to their circle, but will live with thought for the environment. However, most witches are still cautious about using the word 'witch', as prejudice is not unknown.

When embarking on the Craft you do not have to make a final choice at any time. This book is intended as a general grounding in the basics, for almost any path, if you wish to use it that way. If you decide to join a group, do not allow yourself to be influenced by black clothing, occult 'danglies' and charismatic personalities. Go by personal recommendation where possible, and ensure that you feel comfortable and are being empowered and encouraged, not treated as a lowly beginner. Do not expect too much of your teachers, who are not gurus, but earnest seekers who have been on the path longer than you, and try to give help and respect where you can. Leading a coven, or teaching a group, may be thankless and demanding. Reliability, sincerity and kindness are important, on all sides. Perfect love and perfect trust are the witches' ideal.

ETHICS AND RESPONSIBILITY

Because witchcraft has no dogma it should not be assumed that it has no ethics. This is the 'Wytches' Rede':

> *Eight words the witches' creed fulfil*
> *An it harm none, do what you will.*

The archaic wording has a nice ring. 'An' here means 'if', but some have said an older meaning is 'in order that'. This pitches us into the subtle and complex nature of the Rede, concerning exactly what 'harms none'. Could it be that doing what you 'will' (and letting others do likewise) is the best way to avoid harm? History, and often the daily news, reveal that the greatest harm is usually done by those who have a very rigid notion of what is 'right' and seek to coerce or punish those who disagree. By contrast, any harm done by those who are just selfish is quite paltry.

There has been much discussion of the Rede, with some saying you can't possibly 'harm none'. We must avoid entering the realms of the old Medieval debates over how many angels could get together on the top of a pin-head! As far as I am concerned, the Rede means the following:

1 Develop your own 'true will' by listening to the spiritual voice within, and following your path. 'True will' is more than the dictates of the ego: it is the process of becoming what you were meant to be.

2 Harm no other living thing, including yourself. This means having a respect for all of life, but it does not mean that you do not defend yourself, that you repress your righteous anger, or that you feel guilty about eating a lettuce leaf (or meat, if you so choose). It also means that you enjoy the pleasures of life, for not to do so is to 'harm' yourself, and an insult to the Goddess who says, 'All acts of love and pleasure are my rituals'.

Much more could be said on this subject. It's not nearly as simple as being told what you must or must not do, in detail. For instance, what about abortion? Who is being harmed or not harmed here? And what about being unfaithful to your sexual partner? What if you are seriously poor, and you find someone else's purse with £100 inside? The 'Wytches' Rede' is certainly not an invitation to indiscriminate self-indulgence, and it is hardly possible to embrace it sincerely without giving life much thought, and taking responsibility for our actions.

Another occult law that is important to witches has been called 'The Law of Three'. This means that any harm you do to another, through magic, will rebound on you with three times the force you gave out. Some multiply this to three-times-three! However, Doreen Valiente, a much-respected witch and erstwhile associate of Gerald Gardner, states that she believes he made that up, pointing out that there is really no reason for witches to be singled out for special treatment. This makes sense to me. So let us rest simply with the fact that whatever you do comes back to you, be it love or hate, and if you use your magical knowledge to harm another, you will yourself be harmed. Hate someone all you like, for to hate is human, but keep it to yourself – it is your concern and basically your waste of emotional energy! There are those who say there are situations where a curse is justified, such as in the case of the Yorkshire Ripper who murdered so many women. However, magical work done against such a person should, in my view, be a group decision and designed to bring the person to justice, or bind him or her, rather than be an act of vengeance.

My final point about ethics concerns the responsibility to know yourself as well as you can. This may entail undergoing some form of therapy. Witchcraft means accepting your 'dark side' and all your negative emotions for several reasons, not least because they can distort your workings if they are not acknowledged. Accepting this side does not mean indulging it: in fact, it should mean that you are less likely to be subtly controlled by unconscious compulsions. Here there is a power indeed: the power of an integrated personality, the power of transformation, the courage to face yourself. Some say magic and witchcraft are distinct from self-exploration and self-knowledge, but I do not agree, for in the Craft we meet unacknowledged aspects of ourselves more vividly than we do in everyday life. Witches seek 'power to', which means the power of self-determination, creativity, decision and action. They do not seek 'power over', for that panders to the ego, and does not 'harm none'.

FEARS

If you decide that the Craft is for you, however wholeheartedly, it is probable that you will still have fears about your choice. All around us there is an atmosphere of guilt, starting with the concept of Original Sin, and there are few of us who don't have some feeling of guilt at merely being human! It is not a good idea to repress these fears, because magical work will amplify them and send them back to you. It is best to listen to your fears – after all, fear is a survival mechanism. Examine your fears and unravel them. Take your approach to the Craft slowly, with plenty of meditation and pathworking (covered later), working through all that arises in you. A purifying bath prior to rituals, in which you imagine all your fears going down the drain with the water, will also help. However, fears are likely to linger still, for they cling like barnacles, and you can't sweep them out of your circle. The best thing I find is to sit quietly in circle, facing your altar, then bring your fears out with all their teeth and tentacles and lay them before the Goddess. Gaze at the flame of a candle, or into water in your bowl or cauldron. Listen for Her voice within, which is a voice of gentleness and acceptance, and you will find ways to make sense of and deal with fears. Don't rush.

Question yourself If you are thinking of embarking on the path of the witch, now is the time to ask yourself why. What attracts you to witchcraft? What do you hope to achieve? Start as you mean to go on by being very honest. For instance, are you attracted by glamour and power, the need to be 'different' or mysterious? There isn't anything wrong with feeling that way, but hopefully this isn't your only reason! If these are things you want, you need to be aware of the fact so you are not controlled by these motives. (You will find out that it isn't very glamourous when you drop your censer, and that your power is but a drop in the ocean of the Goddess.) List all the benefits you hope for and the inner and outer changes. You can look at these after a while to see whether they still hold good, how many have been achieved, and what now seems irrelevant.

Study It is worth studying some history, for although we do not have definite records, and we are bound to be biased, witchcraft is a tradition, and is rooted in very ancient soil. Anyone who is a witch knows this in their bones. It will give you a better picture of where you are if you know some background. Witchcraft is, after all, about honouring roots and ancestry.

Understand Think about the nature of the Craft. You may like to memorize some words or phrases to describe or defend the Craft to those who question you. Naturally it is also your right to remain silent, for this is your choice. Some witches are more extravert and expressive, while others are very private. You do not have to argue your case or provide intellectual argument for your path. But if you do choose to speak out, it is best to be as coherent as possible.

Your ethics Ethics are very important, and it is good at this point to think about the Rede and what it means to you. Are there situations where you would find it very hard to decide what to do? Think about these. It is okay to be unsure; it is good to take it seriously.

Your notebook   Witches have a notebook in which they keep records and instructions for rituals, important thoughts and realizations, spells, incense recipes etc. This is usually called a Book of Shadows, because it is secret, but also because what is written is but a 'shadow' of reality. Now is the time to start your notebook with some notes on history and ethics.

A gift   Finally, what about a little reward for yourself? Do something you enjoy, as a celebration of life and the gifts of the Goddess.

Suggested books for study   *Witchcraft, A Beginner's Guide, The Goddess: A Beginner's Guide,* Teresa Moorey (Hodder & Stoughton, 1996), *The Language of the Goddess,* Maria Gimbutas (Thames & Hudson, 1989), *Lady of the Beasts,* Buffie Johnson (Inner Traditions International, 1989), *The Book of Goddesses & Heroines,* Patricia Monaghan (Llewellyn, 1993), *An ABC of Witchcraft, Past and Present,* Doreen Valiente (Hale, 1994), *The White Goddess,* Robert Graves (Faber & Faber, 1988)

Finding a group   Resources are listed at the back of the book. The Pagan Federation is comprehensive and helpful. Also look for groups and classes locally, in 'New Age' bookshops, natural therapies clinics or similar. This may take time, and you may have to get to know a few people before you find a suitable group. Look out for anything to do with the Goddess, nature worship, or similar. If you have a local Pagan Moot this will be advertised and is sure to contain witches.

2

GODDESS AND GOD

Goddess and maiden and queen,
be near me now and befriend

SWINBURNE (1837–1909), *HYMN TO PROSERPINE*

THE MEANING OF THE GODDESS

For more than 2,000 years the Goddess has been in exile.
Her temples have been destroyed and Her worshippers
persecuted. However, She needs no temple but the
Greenwood, and no shrine but the heart. The author
Geoffrey Ashe has described a 'goddess-shaped yearning' in
the human spirit, that has been only partially filled by such
figures as the Virgin Mary. Loss of contact with the Goddess
has resulted in many problems, environmentally and
emotionally, because earth is the body of the Goddess and
if you respect Her, instinctively you do not pollute her.
Removal of the Feminine from our concept of divinity has
had far-reaching and profound effects.

Goddess worship is essential to witchcraft, and I have not
heard of a witch who does not honour the Goddess.
Worship of the Goddess does not mean placing a vengeful
Amazon in the clouds, in place of Jehovah, or rewriting the
Book of the Law in a Feminist spirit. It means an approach
that is radically different, free from dogma, rules and
hierarchy. It is important to witches that everyone should
be free to find their own way of worshipping, or not
worshipping, if that is their choice. Worship of the Father
God means obedience, fear and punishment, while worship

of the Goddess means working hard to find your own path and win freedom from fear. The Father God stands for the letter of the law, while Goddess worship seeks the spirit behind it. Inner revelation is the path of the Goddess, but the Father God insists that you follow prophets and priests in an ever-descending hierarchy, the lower echelons thronging with women. In the early centuries of the Church, it was decreed that women had no souls. Women have been regarded as chattels, weak, unstable and dangerous to the morals of righteous men. Menstruation has been demonized and even persecuted, partly no doubt because during menstruation, conception is most unlikely, and the 'child' that then emerges is not a physical one, bearing the surname of the father, but the magical child of the inner creativity, which may threaten cultural norms.

More could be said along these lines, but this is not intended as a diatribe. It is meant to throw into relief certain ingrained attitudes that witches seek to leave behind. We do not realize how deeply our culture is infused with patriarchy, in language and in systems that we accept as normal. For instance, God is always 'He' despite the fact that many thinking people assert that the Deity is, in fact, sexless. The pronoun shouts louder. Eldest sons still inherit; women take on their husbands' name; sexual prejudice dies hard. These aren't the words of a man-hater! I have four sons, have willingly taken my husband's name, and wish I could spend more time 'barefoot, in the kitchen'! However, as we become open to worship of the Goddess, we need to be able to look clearly at the way things are, and to understand how much the Father God and patriarchy linger in us and our surroundings, in a way that has benefited no one, neither men nor women. Witches try to disassemble the 'shoulds' and 'oughts' and to put in their place something more positive and meaningful, and while this may, at times, extend to political issues (depending on the individual), it is far more a matter of inward work.

And so, to the Goddess Herself. She is the substance, the essence, the womb and the tomb. She surrounds us as the star-filled sky, the air and sunlight. Her testimony stands in the stones, and in our own blood, muscle and bones. Her litany calls. She is laid out before us, and yet She is a mystery. She is our 'is-ness', our path to balance and to our own truth. The Jungian psychologist Marion Goodman, quoted in *Caduceus* magazine (Winter, 1997), has a thought-provoking definition of the Goddess:

> *Leaving duality means living in paradox. Paradox is the core of wisdom and the core of the Goddess. Wisdom holds the balance of life/death, mind/body, masculine/feminine. By holding the balance of both, she allows them to transform into something new. Paradox, presence and process are words we associate with the Goddess, she who 'renews everything, while herself perduring'.*

> *This is the judgement of Maat. She does not assign any judgment or rewards for keeping rules or practices. She weighs the heart. If the heart is in balance the process will continue ... In the Old Testament she is wisdom. She is the supreme treasure.*

Maat is the Egyptian goddess of cosmic order. The heart of each deceased person was weighed against Maat, in the form of an ostrich feather, and only if the heart was light with truth could the soul ascend. The heart here is significant, for witchcraft is a way of the heart, not the logical mind, and it is only by aligning ourselves with our centre that we find our own truth.

As the Goddess manifests in our bodies, to those who worship Her, the body is holy. We do not approach the Goddess through mortification of the flesh, but through pleasure and love, including sexual love. Sexuality is sacred and male/female polarity is often thought of by witches as the forces that created the manifest world. While the woman/man union is celebrated, we can be aware that creative polarity exists within homosexual relationships and within the personality of each individual, as well as in many situations, such as when we listen to music, or look at beautiful scenery. The Universe is sexy! Spirituality is not sought through 'rising above' the body and its experiences and needs, but through identifying with it and respecting its wishes. Sensual joy is not a path to evil: it is a celebration of the gifts She has given us. Of course, the Goddess doesn't congratulate us when we are egocentric, greedy and demanding, but She certainly does not demand sacrifice. After centuries of the twisted message that there is something not quite 'nice' about our bodies, and that physical pleasure is inimical to spiritual progress, it is very hard to relax, but it is fun trying!

We saw in Chapter 1 how it is probable that Goddess worship was at one time generally embraced, predating worship of the God by eons. Many stories tell how the primordial Great Mother gave birth to all the other gods. The later removal of the Feminine from the concept of deity has had many implications that go beyond the denigration of women. The words 'matter' and 'mother' have the same root, and rejection of the Goddess has extended to a complete lack of respect for the material world. This is arguably the greatest single factor underlying pollution, factory farming, global warming, deforestation etc. A world that is emptied of the indwelling spirit, and seen in a polarized manner as inferior to the eternal realms, is not good. So while the teaching has been that we should 'rise above' the world and eschew acts of the flesh, in practice the material world has tuned into the demon it was believed to be. People are obsessed with possessing it and subduing it, in a way that is totally out of balance. However, to tell people they must not do something, especially when that something is natural, is a way to ensure that they do it even more, compulsively, despite the threatened consequences.

Goddess worship teaches us that She is present within the world, that She is immanent, not external. All the forces of Nature are sacred, and are there or be celebrated. To enjoy ourselves, to revel in the pleasures of the body and the fruits of the Earth, is a form of worship. Explicitly, sex is included here, as a sacrament of the Goddess. However, to approach these things with lack of respect, in a spirit of exploitation, imbalance and greed, is desecration.

The working of magic derives also from Goddess worship, for worship of the Goddess encourages us to develop our own personal power, to evolve an awareness of other dimensions and to understand that spirit infuses all, even that which is apparently 'inanimate'. Goddess worship, at the heart of witchcraft, comprises respect for all life, the following of our own inner path, direct experiences of the Divine in the world and in our bodies, and an awareness of cycle, celebration, ritual and magic.

From this we should not assume that the Goddess is all hearts and roses, sweet maternal smiles and juicy fruits ripe for the plucking. She is all of these things, but She is more. She is the bitter wind of winter, She is necessity, change, destruction, compost, shit, the bloodied fang. However, this is natural order and it has its value, for life cannot exist without death, and it is death that gives life its meaning. All acts of creation require some destruction in order to bring them about, as any cook or gardener will tell you. The Goddess, in Her dark aspect, does destroy, but She does this in order to bring forth new life. She does not judge and reject, but embraces all as part of Her process and, throughout everything, Her gifts are always that we are comforted, and that we belong.

To most witches the Goddess is first, and to some She reigns virtually alone. I do not think this is through a basic belief in the ascendancy of femaleness, but through a wish for balance. The centuries of neglect of the Goddess mean that we can hardly overdose on Her at present, the only danger here being that Goddess dogmas are erected in place of the Father God. From my perspective, that is to miss the point of Goddess worship. For those of us to whom the Goddess is 'first', this is rather 'first' in order of remembrance, rather than regarding Her as superior in a hierarchical framework. This is a matter of giving respect to our Mother, which is the basis for family and cultural life. Each woman embodies the Goddess, and each man carries Her inside him, as his inner feminine voice, or 'anima'.

MAIDEN, MOTHER AND CRONE

Three important aspects of the Goddess are identified in the witches' trinity, honouring each of the phases of female identity. Patriarchal approaches give some honour to the Mother aspect, as long as She is sexually pure (which is biologically impossible), and virginity also achieves respect, in its denial of the pleasures of sex. In this way feminine power has been castrated and sanitized. Where is the wise old Crone, with all her mother wit? Where is there room to be just a good-enough mother, and a human being besides, in all the self-sacrifice? Where is sexuality and menstruation, the wild woman, the shamanka, the priestess? The Virgin Mary, as the nearest cultural image to the Goddess, does

The Goddess in her triple aspect

not provide a complete, or even possible, role model. Witches have a different outlook.

The Maiden

We may equate the maiden with the idea of being sexually untouched or 'virginal'. However, a very important point is that the word 'virgin' originally had no such meaning, but rather meant a woman who had been possessed by no man. Such a one might be very sexually active, as were the temple virgins, who had sex with travellers as a sacred act, but their behaviour was not controlled by a man. Thus, in her embodiment as the Maiden, the Goddess is as fresh and as free as the March wind. She is full of feminine seductiveness, and is explorative, energetic, an adventuress who embraces experiences but fiercely guards her autonomy. The Goddess, in her aspect as the Maiden, inspires independence, provides challenges, energizes and initiates. Artemis, Athene, Persephone and Eostre are some better-known Maiden goddesses, and the Goddess as Maiden is felt most strongly at Imbolc, the Spring Equinox and Beltane.

The Mother

The Mother is perhaps that most truly loved of all the aspects of the Goddess, for she gives birth to all of the manifest world and pours upon it her blessing. She is present as we produce all of our creative acts, and her understanding, her nourishment and her support are poured out continually upon her children. These include not only humans and animals, but insects, plants, stones, crystals, and everything from the Earth's seething volcanic core out to the furthest stars of the galaxy. In the Mother we understand the meaning of the native American phrase, *mitakuye oyasin*, or 'all my relations', which includes everything that lives, and we realize deep within that we are part of the totality of creation. The Mother is our comforter, for most mother goddesses in mythology lose their son

31

(who, as we shall explore, is also their lover), and the Mother understands loss. The Virgin Mary, mourning beneath Christ's cross, partakes of this tradition. We can see the Mother Goddess giving birth in many different ways, in the summer blooms, the harvest produce and in the rebirth of the Sun at Yule. While she may be especially supportive to human mothers, she is equally a part of every creative act. Some well-known personifications of the Mother Goddess are Demeter, Hera, Cybele and Frigg.

The Crone

Least favourite of the faces of the Goddess is that of the Crone. The medieval witch, when she wasn't disguised as seductress, was a hook-nosed old hag, and many poor old women were hanged, drowned or burnt simply because they were ugly. In a masculine-orientated society, a woman loses just about everything when she passes the age when she can be sexually seductive, and/or have children. The wisdom of the old crone is not something that is culturally valued, and we see beauty only in smooth skin, not in the lines of experience. To witches, the Crone is deeply venerable, for she is mistress of magic, keeper of incommunicable wisdom and guardian of the portals of Otherworld. Here feminine power reaches its zenith. The Crone is healer, keeper of ancestral wisdom, weaver of the fabric of the culture, she who watches, she who knows, holding within her no-longer-menstruating body all the stored experience of our race. She is powerful and transformative. The Crone helps us to deepen our understanding, to make changes, to evolve. The festival at which she is felt most strongly is Samhain, but she stands behind both Maiden and Mother, at Autumn Equinox she peeps in from the threshold, and at the time of greatest darkness, Yule, the Crone is also there. Some well-known faces of the Crone are Sheila-na-Gig, Nokomis and Baba Yaga.

The Goddess, Present and Unseen

As well as the trinity we have just explored, some people also honour a fourth aspect: that of the Goddess, Present and Unseen. If the Crone stands at the entrance to Otherworld, this aspect is its Empress. The Unseen Goddess is the mystery, the stillness at the centre of the hurricane. She is death, reincarnation, rebirth; She is the intergalactic emptiness that was the cradle of all life. For those who meditate upon her, She embodies all those parts of ourselves that we deny or repress, but where our greatest powerhouse is found. Hers is the voice of eternity. This aspect of the Goddess is hard to identify, and merges, sometimes, with the person of the Crone, but is much less consciously accessible. Goddesses who may personify her include Hecate, Gerridwen, Circe and White Buffalo Woman. However, the first two partake also of the Crone, and the second two of the Maiden, to some extent. The Goddess, Present and Unseen is felt especially at Samhain and Yule.

THE CYCLE OF THE SEASONS

It may seem that the Goddess turns different faces towards us as the year turns, for, in the words of the witches' chant, 'She changes everything she touches, everything she touches changes'. A neat classification would be to turn Spring over to the Maiden, Summer to the Mother, Autumn to the Crone and Winter to the Unseen Goddess. However, at any or all of the festivals (which we shall examine in Chapter 6) we may discern two, three or all of the aspects in our observances. Different seasons, different landscapes and types of weather can evoke the Goddess, in one or all of her forms. Of course, the Moon is the most dramatic embodiment of all, Maiden when waxing, Mother when Full, Crone when waning, Present and Unseen when at Dark Moon. The Goddess is ever-present, changeable but constant. One way to understand Her is that She is the cycle, whereas the God travels the cycle, and is equated with the Sun that is 'born' at Yule, grows until Midsummer, and gradually dies as the year wanes, to be born anew at the following Yule. However, in many ancient cultures, including that of the Celts, the Sun was feminine. In contrast, there have been many Moon gods. There is something of a debate about this, but for our purposes here we can continue to think of the Sun as masculine. Naturally, as you reflect and research you may make up your own mind.

THE CHANGE OF THE GODDESS

This is the Goddess invocation, and is used by a great many witches. It was written, using older sources for inspiration, by Doreen Valiente, and is the most total statement of Goddess-belief that I know. Here it is, in its entirety:

> *Whenever ye have need of any thing, once in the month, and better it be when the moon is full, then shall ye gather together in some secret place and adore the spirit of me, who am Queen of all witches. There shall ye assemble, ye who are fain to learn all sorcery, yet have not yet won its deepest secrets; to thee will I teach things that are yet unknown. And ye shall be free from slavery; and as a sign that ye be really free, ye shall be naked in your rites; and ye shall dance, sing, feast, make music and love, all in my praise. For mine is the ecstasy of the spirit, and mine also is joy on earth; for my law is love unto all beings. Keep pure your highest ideal; strive ever towards it; let naught stop you or turn you aside. For mine is the secret door which opens upon the Land of Youth, and mine is the cup of the wine of life, and the Cauldron of Cerridwen, which is the Holy Grail of immortality. I am*

the gracious Goddess, who gives the gift of joy unto the heart of woman. Upon earth I give knowledge of the spirit eternal; and beyond death I give peace, freedom and reunion with those who have gone before. Nor do I demand sacrifice; for behold, I am the Mother of all living, and my love is poured out upon the earth.

In a Wiccan coven the High Priestess recites the Charge. At this point the High Priest interjects:

Hear ye the words of the Star Goddess; she in the dust of whose feet are the hosts of heaven, and whose body encircles the universe.

The High Priestess now continues:

I who am the beauty of the green Earth, and the white Moon among the stars, and the mystery of the waters, and the desire of the heart of man, call unto thy soul. Arise, and come unto me. For I am the soul of Nature, who gives life to the universe. From me all things proceed and to me all things must return; and before my face, beloved of gods and of men, let thine innermost divine self be enfolded in the raptures of the infinite. Let my worship be within the heart that rejoiceth; for behold, all acts of love and pleasure are my rituals. And therefore let there be beauty and strength, power and compassion, honour and humility, mirth and reverence within you. And thou who thinkest to seek for me, know they seeking and yearning shall avail thee not unless thou knowest the mystery; that if that which thou seekest thou findest not within thee, thou wilt never find it without thee. For behold, I have been with thee from the beginning; and I am that which is attained at the end of desire.

THE GOD

I once heard someone saying, 'It's against God's law to hang out washing on a Sunday', and I couldn't help muttering, 'That God needs a wife!' The witches' God does not make laws and stand apart. He is a playboy and a lover, a hero, guardian, king and sacrifice. He is Lord of the Dance, and embodies joy in life. He impregnates; he has movement and purpose. His sword, a metaphor for the conscious, logical mind, is used to differentiate between what is valuable and what is a waste of time, to 'cut through the crap' but not to terrorize and subdue. In some ways the God of the witches is in service to the Feminine, not as a hen-pecked sidekick, but as a proud and brave defender of the mysteries. He is the Horned God of Nature, both the hunter and the hunted, and his horns are at once an embodiment of his own phallic power and a salute to the Moon and the curving fallopian tubes of the female reproductive system.

The God is also playful. He is the trickster, the sacred fool, and in so being He pushes back the doors of perception. While the Goddess is ever-changing, She is constant. The God has a quality of unpredictability that shocks and awakens. His animal exuberance drives Him, but his quest is high and deep, and in following it, He shows us pathways to spirit, through change to rebirth. We may think of the Goddess as the cycle itself, while the God travels the cycle.

It seems that representations of the God came later in history than the more ancient Goddess images. Cave paintings in Spain and France, created 12,000 years ago, show a horned hunting god, half man and half animal. These figures seem to show the 'myth of the hunter' that rose up alongside the 'myth of the Goddess'. As Cashford and Baring explore in *The Myth of the Goddess* (see Further Reading), the Goddess myth may include the hunter, but

The Horned God

the hunter myth cannot embrace the Goddess. In other words, the instinctual state of being where there is participation in Nature can contain life and death, as it does, and even rupture of the continuum is, paradoxically, a part of it. This state may equate with what is believed to be the earliest phase of humanity, as hunter-gatherers. As hunting grew in importance, so images and rituals evolved for those who ruptured the continuum, by killing, and these may have involved sacrifice as propitiation. At the same time, on another level, a greater consciousness of individual ego was possibly growing, along with alienation from the spiritual source. The God, who is god of the hunt, god of the herded animal and, later, god of vegetation, parallels the journey of the ego, emerging from an instinctual unity to follow its quest for individuality, returning again to its source for rebirth. This is more than a metaphor for human life: it is a symbol of spiritual awakening, which some say is to blossom in the Age of Aquarius. To paraphrase T.S. Eliot, we find that at the end of our exploration we are back where we started, but seeing the place for the first time. As humans, we came out of the dream time into centuries of striving, and our homecoming shall hopefully be that we return to our source, yet bringing our individuality and our consciousness with us, to reach some as yet unimaginable new state. The story of our awakening is the story of the God's passage.

This is taking us somewhat ahead of ourselves, however. For witches the God is seen as going through life and earth, and finding rebirth. His journey is paralleled by the annual journey of the Sun. The Wiccan god is called Cernunnos, or Karnayna, the Horned One. The early Christian church turned him into the devil, for Christianity feared the darkness of the group mind and the Dionysian revels, and was part of the human drive to strengthen the Apollonian approach of the rational, separate consciousness. However, as recently as the thirteenth century, a priest in Inverkeithing in Scotland was taken to task for leading his parishioners in a dance around a phallic figure. Nonetheless, he was not deprived of his position, thanks to a sympathetic bishop who may have instinctively appreciated the value in his approach.

THE GOD'S YEARLY STORY

The God, born of the Goddess at Yule, is shown as young and phallic at Imbolc, and mating with the Goddess at Spring Equinox or Beltane. We should note that some traditions derive from the Continent, where warm weather comes early, and to some pagans Spring Equinox is principally a festival of the fertility of vegetation, which is, of course, personified by the God. We may choose to emphasize either of the Spring festivals as the mating of Goddess and God; however, Beltane features sexual delight and fulfilment. We see the young God growing to maturity and taking His place beside the now pregnant Goddess as Her consort and protector. In such a way the God attains maturity and responsibility, moving from Lord of the Greenwood to Sun King. This is an image of the experience of many human males who move into a new phase of responsibility through their relationship with a woman, but it also means the inward journey of a man as he learns to

listen to his feminine side, or his anima, and becomes more
rounded. For a woman, following the journey of the God
can also foster internal balance, as she becomes conscious
of her inner masculinity, or animus, helping her to make
distinctions, to think and to assert herself. This is not to say
that the Goddess is not inherently fierce and assertive, but
masculine assertion has a more focused quality, with a
designated purpose, and many women feel it is important
to develop this.

At Lammas/Lughnasadh the sacrifice of the God as Corn
King fertilizes the land. This was acted out in true ritual
sacrifice in times gone by. In terms of human life it signifies
the need to let go of what must go in order to evolve.
The God now embarks on the quest of the Hero, which
symbolizes the journey of the ego into the shadowlands of
the unconscious. Tales of heroic quests parallel the struggles
of the ego when faced with the terrifying contents of the
unconscious mind, which actually transform and renew
when they are integrated. In *Memories, Dreams, Reflections*
(Flamingo, 1985) C.G. Jung describes a dream he had,
which revealed to him the meaning of the hero archetype:

> *I grasped the stone ... and discovered a hollow
> underneath ... there was running water. In it a corpse
> floated by, a youth with blond hair and a wound in the
> head. He was followed by a gigantic black scarab and
> then by a red, newborn sun rising up out of the depths
> of the water ... I realized, of course, that it was a hero
> and solar myth, a drama of death and renewal, the
> rebirth symbolized by the Egyptian scarab ...*

This account illustrated the hero's death, and the promise of
renewal, guiding us through our own endings, sacrifices
and transformations. The God goes into the Underworld,
re-emerging at the Autumn Equinox to reclaim the Goddess
who reigns beside Him in the Underworld at Samhain.
Eventually the God is released into the transcendent, as His

son, born at Yule, now grows to take His place, and the cycle begins anew. The Goddess, in a sense, is also reborn, for She rebirths Herself as Maiden, and while we speak of the God as Son/Lover, here there is no implication of literal incest. At Imbolc the God and Goddess are both youthful once more. Here, in this cyclic 'love story' we find ways to cope with the cycles, changes and losses in our own lives.

Many men enter witchcraft, or Wicca, with the wish to find their 'feminine' side, and most pagan men are to be found looking after children and doing their part in home and kitchen. However, while this is laudable and necessary, the point here is that masculinity should not be lost, but strengthened. Men may grow through a phase of possible subservience into a more rounded, powerful expression of masculinity, where the inner voice of the unconscious feminine, the anima, is heard. Here a man can give space to his feelings, without becoming overwhelmed by them, and be made more solid, more human and possessed of greater conviction. Of course we can all partake of the Goddess and God, but for women the Goddess is usually more accessible, while the God is closer for the majority of men. However, they are both within each of us, and within the natural world.

OAK KING AND HOLLY KING

The God has many aspects, but the polarities emerge as Oak King and Holly King, Lord of the Waxing Year and Lord of the Waning Year respectively. Inside the annual drama are the twice-yearly battles between these two powers. At Midsummer, Holly King wins as the darkness begins to overwhelm the light, and at Yule, Oak King wins, as light gains in power. Here we have two aspects of the God, Father and Son. One can be seen as representing decay and destruction, the precursor to new growth, and also the hidden realms of wisdom. The other stands for effectuality, presence in the external world, drive and expansion. As Lord of Light, the God embodies all that is vibrant; as Lord of Death, He is our solace, and in this guise He is also rune-master and magician. Wiccans celebrate and re-enact the Oak/Holly struggle in rituals at Midsummer and Yule. This story is present in several myths, including that of the Green Knight in Arthurian legend. The Green Knight begs to be slain, must be slain, yet can never be totally vanquished. Always the old king must give way to the new, or we have tyranny and stagnation: the father must give way to the son. Life must change, death means life, and life means death. The French encapsulate it in the phrase *plus ça change, plus c'est la même chose.*

MANY MEANINGS

As we meditate upon the Goddess and God, different aspects emerge, different perspectives are revealed, symbolism deepens and meanings widen. The myths of the 'Old Ones' have both psychological and spiritual meanings, but they are also a background to celebration and a dramatization of the natural cycles through which we, and all of Nature, travel. These stories are not something that one 'believes' in, although they possess an abiding truth, for witches do not tend to 'believe' in a literal fashion, but seek more to experience, to deepen and to evolve. On this note, the idea of reincarnation is one that most witches embrace in some form. As Nature is born again, so are we, and the phrase 'Once a witch, always a witch' may be taken to refer to successive lifetimes.

MANY GODDESSES AND GODS

We have looked at the Goddess and God in terms of their yearly story, for they are venerated in eight festivals throughout the year, as we shall explore in Chapter 6. However, witches honour the Goddess and God in many different forms, drawing upon Greek, Celtic, Norse and Egyptian pantheons, and more. This is because no one form can encompass all aspects of divinity, at least not in a relevant and vivid manner, and so witches use different images of much-loved goddesses and gods to draw closer to the Divine. This is called 'polytheism'. 'Pantheism', which means 'God is in everything', is also a relevant notion, for witches see the Goddess as immanent. 'Animism', which means 'everything is alive', has been called a primitive outlook, but it is, in fact, profoundly spiritual, and to witches all the world is alive as different vibrations on a spectrum. This is central to magic. As witches we move comfortably through animism, pantheism, polytheism and Goddess/God approaches, and sometimes all of this may be present in one ritual. Finally, we may attempt to be philosophically correct by saying that 'It's all one divinity anyway' and in a sense that too is true, for the Goddess and God can be seen as emanating from a single unknowable Source, called by Qabalists the 'Ain Soph'. Perhaps our route is, ultimately, union with this Source and an end to polarity-consciousness. If so, the Goddess and the God stand at the portals to enlightenment, showing us the way.

Finally, a word about gender stereotypes. These are a way of talking about life, but are not meant to confine personal identity or expression. If you do not like the descriptions given here, explore your own.

TRAINING SESSION 2

Reflect   Gather together your thoughts on the Goddess and the God. Do they vary from what I have described? Reflect also on the effects of patriarchy culturally, and in your own life. What difference can worship of the Goddess make? What does it mean to you? (Note here feelings and impressions of all types, not just what seems 'logical'.) How might you bring Her closer? In following chapters we shall explore the significance of the eight seasonal festivals and the Moon in this context, but for now you may like to make some notes of your own. Take time over this to deepen your own awareness, and form your viewpoint, which, naturally, you may choose to change later.

Study   Research some different aspects and forms of goddesses and gods. I suggest the following: Bride, Cerridwen, Rhiannon, Blodeuedd, Persephone and Demeter, Isis and Osiris, Freya/Frigg, Kali, Hecate, Lugh, Shiva, Fionn mac Cumhail, Orpheus, Pan, Cernunnos, Gaia and Ouranos.

Suggested books for study   Two simple books to start with are *The Goddess: A Beginner's Guide* and *Pagan Gods: A Beginner's Guide, Teresa Moorey* (Hodder & Stoughton, 1997). Following this you may try some or all of the following: *The Witches' Goddess* and *The Witches' God*, Janet and Stewart Farrar (Phoenix, 1987 & 1989 respectively), *Voices of the Goddess*, Caitlin Matthews (Aquarian, 1990), *Goddesses for Every Season*, Nancy Blair (Element, 1995), *The Ancient British Goddess*, Kathy Jones (Ariadne, 1991), *The Crone Oracles*, Ransom & Bernstein (Weiser, 1994), *The Thirteen Original Clan Mothers*, Jamie Sams (HarperCollins, 1994), *Wicca: the Old Religion in the New Age* (especially the chapter on the God), Vivianne Crowley (Aquarian, 1989), *His Story*, Nicholar Mann (Llewellyn, 1995)

3

SACRED SPACE

Is it not your breath that has erected and
hardened the structure of your bones?
And is it not a dream which none of you
remember having dreamt, that builded your
city and fashioned all there is in it?
Could you but see the tides of that breath you
would cease to see all else,
And if you could hear the whispering of the
dream you would hear no other sound.

KAHLIL GIBRAN, *THE PROPHET* (1923)

THE SACRED ALL ROUND

We have seen that the Goddess and the God are with us and around us, always, immanent in Earth and sky. To witches this isn't a theory or an article of faith but a beautiful and enveloping reality. When you look at a windswept hill you are looking at the Goddess: Her tears fall in the rain, Her heartbeat is in the breast of each little brown bird that hops and flies, every forest is Her temple, every hearth Her altar. If you are drawn to witchcraft you are sure to resonate with this, for every witch is in some sense a 'Nature mystic' even if you are a city-dweller. The ordinary world isn't 'ordinary' at all: it is sacred, magical, exciting. It is the breath of the Great Mother.

Almost certainly ancient people were well in touch with these matters. The Celts, for instance, had a vivid sense of the sacredness of space, as a metaphor for the world of spirit. This is a different mindset from that which is general today, where the material world is either looked upon as being the only reality, or as being inferior, dull and empty, compared with spiritual realms. To witches, spirit and matter are not split but are variations along the same spectrum. The idea of the sacredness of space and the sacredness of the land was retained thoroughly by the Irish Celts, who were not Romanized. The land was Goddess and the High King derived His authority from the land. This was specifically honoured in a ceremony where the king, as part of his coronation, mated with a mare, who personified the Goddess. Many specific goddesses were associated with horses, such as Macha, Rhiannon and Epona. This 'sacred marriage' was also consummated, in different places at different times, by a mating between king and High Priestess. The linking of the land with Goddess was most pervasive, and one of the symbols for Egyptian Isis was the throne, signifying that he who ruled did so by Her authority. This theme lingers in Arthurian legend, where the land is laid waste after Arthur has become estranged from Guinvere (who, despite her later trivialization, was a Goddess-aspect) and can only be restored by the finding of the Holy Grail, the Grail or chalice being a feminine symbol.

The Irish Celts were quite literal about the symbolic nature of their land, quartering it, as we do the magic circle (to be explored in the following chapter). Leinster, in the East, was allied to life, air, Spring, and dawn, and its symbol was the sword (or arrow). Munster, in the South, was linked to light, fire, Summer, noon and spear (or rod). Connaught in the West was love, water, Autumn, evening and cauldron (or cup). Ulster in the North was for law, earth, Winter, night and stone (or shield, or mirror). The four elements included here were/are united by the subtle and pervasive element of ether, represented geographically by Meath, the central seat of kingship, where stood royal Tara. However, more than this, in common with many so-called 'primitives', including the Native Americans, the Celts saw everyday life as a spiritual experience, all simple acts having symbolic significance, being in a sense acts of worship. Most of us are aware of this at some level, and even the most prosaic person can see that turning out one's cupboards, for instance, can clear one's mind. But there is more to it than this, and to find it, simply go out into park or garden, field or woodland, and invite it into your soul.

GOING TO THE CENTRE

At Tara stood the centre, the seat of sovereignty, where the mind met the land. This was also classically known as the *omphalos* or naval, and a stone at the Greek temple of Delphi was thought of as marking the centre of the world, where the flight paths of two great eagles released by Zeus crossed. However, an omphalos stone was part of the ground plan of many ancient ceremonial sites and is echoed today in the laying of foundation stones for buildings. The symbolism is obvious: the navel is the point through which we received our earliest sustenance, our primal 'earthing' and the meeting of our spirit with its incarnation. However, in *The Wise Wound* (see Further Reading), Shuttle and Redgrove also link the omphalos with the cervix, or birth cone, through which we emerge into the world. Either way, the omphalos or sacred centre is our contact with the spiritual planes.

Linked to the omphalos is the cosmic axis, or World Tree. The most well-known World Tree is Yggdrasil, from Norse mythology, connecting Lower World, Middle World and Upper World in its roots, trunk and branches. The idea of the World Tree is used as a kind of cosmic map, especially for shamanic journeying. Shamanism is the art of spirit flight, probably practised by all ancient peoples in some form, and shamans were active in the spirit world, guiding the souls of the dead and obtaining information to help hunters and chieftains. The three worlds of many shamanic cosmologies are Upper, Middle and Lower, each containing specific types of entities or sources of power. Upper World is that of sky divinities, of panoramic perspectives, Lower World the ancestral power-house and Middle World the realm of elemental spirits, closest to our everyday experience. (This subject is more fully outlined in *Shamanism: A Beginner's Guide*, see Further Reading.) While much shamanism is believed to have been concerned with success in the hunt, thus esoterically linking the shaman with the wild creatures involved, it is quite probable that the first shamans were women, for women are often able to 'shamanise' more instinctively. Also each woman, through her 'wise wound' of menstruation, carries the wounding or 'sickness' characteristic of shamanism, often as extreme as near-death experience, through which a gateway to spirit became available. While much modern shamanic journeying is based on North American beliefs and practices, witchcraft is essentially a shamanic tradition, with its emphasis on trance and experience of Otherworld. Arguably, the traditions of the witch draw on sources that are in the bones of many people of Caucasian descent. In addition there are many links between Celtic practices (which underlay much of witchcraft) and the spirituality of the Indian subcontinent, including some similarities of language.

SACRED SITES

There are many sites around the globe especially designated as 'sacred'. These extend from Glastonbury, Avebury, Callanish, Carnac and the many stone circles of the British Isles and Europe to Native American sites, lines on the landscape of South America and the ancestral songlines in Australia, where the earth was 'sung' into being and is repeatedly trod and resung by Aborigines, so

The landscapes of Europe are scattered with ancient, magic stone circles, such as the Castlerigg Stone Circle in Cumbria.

affirming the continually creative nature of the magical and tender bond between humans and our planet.

Energies within the Earth, its sacredness, the way our ancestors related to it, and the way we resonate with the land, forms a subject in itself, covered in *Earth Mysteries: A Beginner's Guide* (see Further Reading). To witches, the sentience within the Earth and the many energies pulsing therein are a reality. Sites such as Avebury in England, whatever their many uses and whatever their undoubted astronomical and other significances, to us seem self-evidently ceremonial in nature, and as such are being reclaimed by present-day pagans. It is quite possible to sense for yourself the awesome nature of these spots, and you may choose to go at times when there will be few others around in order to experience the atmosphere.

Take dowsing rods, if you like, but nothing is truly necessary to connect you, other than an open heart and mind. Rather than travelling to the well-known sites, it may be better to discover what you can about your locality, for certainly in the British Isles there is no shortage of standing stones, barrow mounds, holy wells and springs. Failing this, seek out your own sacred grove, your secret spot by hedge, riverside, hilltop. Just go, look, breathe, and be.

OTHERWORLD

Otherworld is always with us. In moments of stillness we glimpse its silver shadows. Otherworld glimmers in dewdrops and rainbows. Its occupants flit at the corners of our vision, its entrances are found by moonlight, in the barrow mound, the hallowed grove, by the enchanted lake. To the Celts, Otherworld was a kind of heavenly place peopled by the Sidhe (pronounced 'shee') or people of Faerie, gods and heroes, or the Tuatha de Danaan, the magical race that preceded the Celts and now dwell within the mysterious mounds of earth, built in time-before-time. The Tuatha did not die, but slid into another dimension, as so much is believed to have done, as we erased it from our mind-maps by ceasing to believe. For 'reality' is no crystallized structure; it is merely data from our five senses, censored by the brain. We say, 'Seeing is believing' but believing is also seeing, as also *not* believing is *not* seeing.

We may think of Otherworld in a variety of ways. Probably it equates best with the idea of Middle World, which is the ordinary world, in a sense, seen with expanded vision. This world is peopled by many spirits, elemental beings, devas and faeries. We might also think of it as the next 'dimension'. It is a magical place in many senses. Anything magical that we do has its being first in Otherworld. It can also be referred to as the astral plane, and order of existence, vibrating at a higher rate than our own. It is a world of finer essence, that we may enter each night, in our dreams, or purposely, in states of trance. We all possess an astral body, interpenetrating our physical, which may separate when we sleep, or 'astral travel' in trance states. Some occultists state that we have many astral bodies, vibrating at ever-higher rates and equating with various levels of the astral plane. The accounts of witches' flights, on the symbolic broomstick, are probably accounts of astral travelling, and the broomstick may well mean a branch of the World Tree that forms shamanic cosmology. Magical effects first take shape on the astral plane.

It is important for witches to have some sense of Otherworld. This does not mean that we have to be literal about our cosmological maps and what fits where, but a concept of Otherworld, or more subtle states of being, are basic to the outlook and the art of the witch, and are part of our poetry, our reality and our devotion. While many witches have had experiences of Otherworld and its occupants, in varying degrees of vividness, there are indeed others who apparently have little or no direct feeling for Otherworld. I do not think that this precludes witchdom, as long as there is acceptance and openness. However, it does mean that rituals need to be conducted with extra care with regard to protection and grounding, if more subtle senses cannot be relied upon to flag up what is necessary. In time, these subtle senses usually grow. If you don't feel a sense of Otherworld there could be lots of reasons for this. It may be that you are strongly 'sensation function' as we shall explore in the next chapter, focused on your physical senses and practicialities. However, it is arguably the farmers and the practical people who have the most literal experience of ghostly happenings and you may one day have an encounter that will amaze you. It may also be that your rational mind is filtering out some experiences, and even that your unconscious fears are keeping them at bay.

You may need to take more care with your training than a more 'natural' witch, but if you feel deep inside that the path is for you, you will find your way to it.

THE MAGIC CIRCLE

The foregoing all forms a background to the witches' magic circle. Again, many witches will know instinctively how to cast a circle. However, such information can help to keep our logical minds happy while instinct gets on with the job. The magic circle is the place within which all ritual and magical endeavour takes place. The centre of each magic circle is, in a sense, the omphalos where spirit meets matter, where matter meets spirit. It is formed by mind-stuff, using ritual to strengthen the process. Literally, it is made from the etheric energy from the body of the witch or witches, and may be discerned by occultists. Other witches may have differing ideas, but to me the purpose of the circle is three-fold.

1 It contains the power raised by the ritual until the time for release. In this way energy is not unwittingly dissipated.
2 It protects the witch from any elementals or other entities that are attracted to the ritual, for a powerful working may light a kind of astral beacon to which strays may be attracted.
3 It forms a type of half-way house, a world-between-the-worlds, where Otherworld may be impinged upon.

Strictly speaking the circle is not really a circle, but a sphere with three dimensions. Nor does the circle have to be literally 'circular' as a witch may cast the circle around the perimeters of the room. However, the symbolism of the circle as a perfect geometrical shape is very important, for it partakes of infinity. Simply, it is something to which we instinctively turn.

I feel it is most important to get the hang of the magic circle, especially if you are working alone, for it is an important boundary. The circle tells us when and where magical consciousness is appropriate, and where it is not. Some people become removed when they become involved with the occult, or take up witchcraft. This can be modified by properly forming the circle, and by dissipating and grounding, at the right time. In addition, forming the circle is a very important visualization exercise. An experienced witch can 'throw' a circle around her/himself in an instant, and this can be a help in ordinary life. For instance a witch friend of mine who is very striking looking totally averted being noticed by someone whom she needed to avoid, by putting a circle around herself, despite the fact that the person passed within a yard of her.

A 'mini' version of the magic circle is achieved by imagining oneself inside a protective bubble. If you do this regularly your 'bubble' will become stronger and stronger. Don't forget to disperse it, or you may find that you become disconnected from other people and from daily life. This bubble, thought of by some as a golden sphere, can be a great help when entering mundane situations that feel threatening. You can visualize this bubble as essentially an egg shape, surrounding your body, in which case it is a strengthened version of your aura, or you may extend it by a metre or two. I would recommend putting a circle in place when doing anything ritualistic, meditation or trancework, in short, anything that has any references to Otherworld, and also when you need to be protected from anything or anyone.

Traditionally the occultists' magic circle is 9 feet in diameter, formed by a cord $4^1/_2$ feet long, secured at the centre and stretched out to form the circumference. These measurements are not arbitrary. They are based on symbolism and the measurements of the megalithic culture, and while you are quite at liberty to have a circle of different dimensions (and practicality may dictate this), please do not casually substitute metric measurement. Some people like to mark out the circle on the floor, and this is fine if you have a special room set aside as your temple. Or the circle could be marked beneath a rug, which is removed for the occasion. A circular rug could itself form the perimeter, if you wish. If you are not very good at visualizing, do not hesitate to use whatever props you like. Initially your circle can be formed by closing your eyes and imagining it as a circle of blue light. If other senses are more easily brought to play, use them. For instance, you may 'feel' your circle as a tingling perimeter, hear it humming like a power circuit, or smell it, like frankincense, in the air around you. Simply, you may get a feeling of safety and security.

In full ritual the circle may be cast with sword or athame (see Chapter 5), or with your fingertip. Sword and athame are covered in Chapter 5. They are a way of focusing your energy and cutting 'reality'. You may find your finger works as well. I think it is best to use your leading hand, usually the right hand (but use the left if you are left-handed), for this is an action of consciously directing energy and making an effort of will, rather than opening to the receptivity of the unconscious. Imagine a blue light issuing from the tip of your finger or athame. If you have opened your chakras this will flow better, and many witches do this automatically. Instructions on the chakras are given in Chapter 8. Construct your circle *deosil*, which means 'in the direction of the Sun', starting in the North. This is an appropriate direction for positive matters. Deosil is clockwise in the northern hemisphere, anti-clockwise in the southern, although some witches in Australia do decide to operate as if they were in the northern hemisphere, where the practices originated.

The sacred space of your circle must be cleansed, and this is done symbolically with the aid of a besom. You may sweep out your circle before you cast it, or after. I don't think it matters which method you use. As you sweep, imagine all negativity and any irrelevancies of the day-to-day world being cast out. This will include distractions from your own mind. You can imagine this as grey clouds that you are sweeping away. Of course, you do not have to use a besom, you may just sweep out the unneccessaries with your hands. When you have finished stay still for a moment or two and check that all feels clear. Affirm that your sacred space is pure and cleansed, ready for your workings. A chant that you might use while sweeping is:

> *Broom of rowan, pure and strong*
> *Fight the battle between right and wrong*
> *Cleanse the circle, unite us all*
> *Lest evil forces take their toll.*

Personally, I don't like references to right and wrong, for witchcraft is not a path of polarity and strife, nor do I like to end with a reference to 'evil forces'. I prefer simply to say:

> *Cleansed be, safe be*
> *Any badness leave thee.*

Of course, you do not have to say anything at all, if you prefer not to, but words are a powerful vehicle to back up intent.

The circle is also consecrated by salt and water, as the elements of Earth and Water. Fire and Air are also used in consecration too. These elements are specifically invoked at the Four Quarters, as we shall be examining in the next chapter. However, salt and water have a specific part to play in the purification of the sacred space. Place your finger, or athame, over a chalice or bowl of water and form a pentagram (see Chapters 4 and 5) or form the pentagram in the water. Then say, 'May this water be blessed, in the name of the Lady and the Lord'. Do similarly with the salt: add the salt to the water, stirring it with finger or athame and sprinkle it deosil around your circle. You may sprinkle salt and water separately, if you prefer. After this your circle is ready for you to invoke the elements, or Watchtowers, an explanation of which is given in the following chapter.

Once constructed, it is possible to come in and out of your circle, if you need to. Try to keep this to the minimum, however. Proper preparation for your ritual should include going to the lavatory beforehand! Do not simply pass through, but consciously open a doorway and close it behind you, using your athame, if you have one, or just your finger. In a Wiccan coven someone will do this for you and will welcome you back over the threshold with a kiss. Small children and animals can pass in and out of the circle freely, for they do not disrupt the etheric energy. However, for various reasons, it will not be suitable to have young children present for most rituals. Pets may be drawn to magical workings, especially cats, and there is no harm at all in their presence, probably the reverse, if it does not distract you.

YOUR ALTAR

Personal altars in the home give focus to your own ritual and magic

55

As the circle is sacred space, the altar is the devotional and working focus within it. It is usually placed in the North of the circle, because North is associated with the element of Earth, the most basic of the elements, and North is the dark side of the sky, foreign to Sun and Moon, and witchcraft is a path of instinct and nighttime. Witches in the southern hemisphere may choose to place their altar in the South, for the same reasons.

The altar is covered more fully in Chapter 5. On it you will honour all the elements, the Goddess and the God, and place seasonal offerings, if your ritual is to celebrate one of the Sabbats. In addition you can put on your altar any other equipment for specific spells or activities such as scrying (see Chapter 9). If, like most people, you do not have the room in your home to keep separate a room for rituals, your altar could be a folding table. A coffee table or large box will also do, covered by an appropriate cloth.

CLOSING DOWN

Your circle is composed of your etheric energy, the stuff of your mind and spirit. After you have completed your rites, the circle must be consciously allowed to fade. What is happening is that the energy is being reabsorbed by you. Wiccans may reabsorb the energy through the point of the athame, while they form the 'banishing pentagrams' in the air (these are discussed in the following Chapter 7). However you approach this it is important that the circle should be closed down thoroughly. You can do this just by standing still and mentally drawing all back within. Part of the process is saying farewell to the Guardians and closing down the portals to Otherworld. You may simply hold out your arms and draw them back against your breast, then touch the ground with your palms to signify all is earthed. The importance of closing down needs to be stressed, as you will feel depleted and too 'open' if you do not do it thoroughly. Chakras, if they are opened, need to be closed, any remaining energy grounded and contact reaffirmed with the everyday world. Eating and drinking help this; patting yourself, stamping and placing palms flat on the ground will also help. Naturally, in any place where ritual has been powerfully and repeatedly performed, there will be a strong, lingering atmosphere, and that is all to the good, for it makes the resumption of ritual and magic flow more freely.

Practice   Practise forming and dispersing your protective circle regularly. Devote a few minutes to this each day, until you feel confident that you are able to do it. Some people ask, 'How will I know I have done it properly, and how will I know it is gone?' Probably you will feel a confidence in this developing, as you practise. If this sense does not come easily to you, keep trying. If you affirm clearly and definitely, using props if you like, and if you affirm equally clearly that the force of the circle has been reabsorbed, then the chances are very much that this has happened. In witchcraft, as you will, so shall it be. If you are not doing it properly, you will feel strange, and it is better that you should be conscious of it at this stage rather than progress to more complex rituals. If you do feel odd, review your closing and grounding efforts. Sometimes, as was mentioned earlier, the circle works to make you temporarily 'invisible'. However, I would not advise doing this in an experimental way, or to acquire 'proof'. Practise also strongly visualizing your circle before going into different situations. You should notice a difference in the way you feel and cope.

Nature   Spend time alone with Nature, reinforcing your connection with the natural world. You may do specific things, such as hugging a tree, communing with the spirit of a tree, or dowsing with rods or pendulums. You may go so far as to sleep out in the crop circle or near a barrow, but do not undertake these activities lightly, for they can be scary, and of course do not expose yourself to any danger. You may just go out for regular walks, simply noticing your surroundings and not doing anything special at all. It is a fairly well-accepted fact that contact with the natural world aids all psychic powers and may work much better than a candlelit chamber in awakening you to Otherworld.

Your altar   In order to enhance your contact with the sacred, erect an altar or shrine in your home to the Goddess. A shrine differs, in my opinion, from an altar, in that an altar is a less permanent, more dynamic working space, while a shrine is a testament. Your shrine may be as simple or as complex as you wish. You can place statues and pictures of the Goddess in any guise you wish there, and many lovely effigies can be bought in New Age shops. Flowers, acorns, pine-cones, corn-dollies, and seasonal greenery can all be placed there too, along with a candle or candles and any other symbolic or attractive artefact that seems suitable. Your altar should be tended at least weekly. You may burn incense or place offerings, which you later return to the earth (such as seeds, bread or anything seasonal). At different times you may wish to place different images there, for instance at Samhain you may choose to place a photograph of a departed relative. We shall be looking at making an altar specifically to the Moon in Chapter 7, and the seasonal festivals are covered in Chapter 6. For now, your purpose is to make a sacred space, so you may more fully experience this meaning for yourself. If you do not have privacy, why not clear a shelf in a cupboard, to devote as your altar?

Pathworking   The craft of the witch takes place on the inner planes, and arguably your most important activity as a witch is pathworking. Pathworking is a type of inner journey. However, the word 'inner' does not mean that you disappear inside yourself, but very much the reverse, for you are going beyond the confines of the ego, beyond the day-to-day world, into the realms of the collective, which the psychologist C.G. Jung termed 'the collective unconscious'. The collective unconscious is replete with powerful symbols and archetypes, and can in a sense be equated with the astral plane, although there is also more to the astral plane. These are subtle matters. Existence is on many levels, apart from the physical and it may be inappropriate to be categorical concerning definitions. However, when I travel spiritually I am aware of a connection with the oceanic realms of the collective, but also of forces and entities that are far above this. Spirit travel is real. It can reveal much to you about yourself, and this is one of the reasons that witchcraft is allied to self-knowledge. It will also open you inspirationally, generally and particularly, and may at times provide literal answers.

The terms 'pathworking', 'guided visualization', 'meditation', 'inner journeying' and others may be used more or less interchangeably. Meditation, in this sense, is not quite the mind-emptying exercise common to Eastern disciplines, but a process of centering, and going within. These terms are perhaps best understood as variations upon a spectrum. When you undertake shamanic journeys you have no guidance except the purpose of your journey, which you may take against the background of a drumbeat, or silently. At the other end of the scale comes guided visualization, where someone else, either in person or on a tape, takes you through the inward stages. Pathworking tends to come somewhere in between, where the inner landscapes are mapped. Some pathworkings are more detailed than others. They are intended to take you on a specific journey to an internal destination. Some are allied to the Jewish doctrine of the Qabbalah. However, this is not really the same as guided visualization, which is usually designed to produce specific results, such as greater relaxation.

Pathworking is more focused on opening the inner eye to extended reality. The paths you will work are the paths of Otherworld.

If you are not at all experienced at pathworking, here is a simple exercise, passed to me by our illustrator, Jane Brideson, that you can undertake as a start. Begin by doing it once a week at first. When you feel at ease, which may happen very quickly, you may then do it more frequently, although it may be preferable to move on to more extended workings, which we shall meet later in the book.

> *Sit or lie comfortably, close your eyes and relax. Allow a feeling of peace to come over you. Imagine that you are standing in front of a curtain.*
>
> *Slowly the curtain is drawn back, revealing a beautiful scene in nature. Over a panorama of hills the sun gently shines. A soft breeze blows the scent of blossom towards you. The grass is emerald green. Butterflies flutter and bees gather honey from the clover. Overhead, birds are winging. Trees stretch their branches towards the sky. All is peace and beauty.*
>
> *Stand before this scene for a while, noticing the colours and the shapes, breathing in the scents, noting all the sounds of the countryside. Pause for a while.*
>
> *Now the curtain slowly draws back into place again. Come back into the everyday world in your own time. Centre yourself and ground yourself by touching your body, touching the ground, eating and drinking. This has been a sight of Otherworld.*

When you are more experienced, or if you feel ready, you may like to enter the scene to experience more. But for now this simple exercise will suffice to begin your connection to Otherworld.

Be sure to note all your experiences and feelings in your notebook.

4

THE ELEMENTS

Among the mythological representations of the Self one finds much emphasis on the four corners of the world, and in many pictures the Great Man is represented in the centre of a circle divided into four. Jung used the word 'mandala' (magic circle) to designate a structure of this order, which is a symbolic representation of ... the human psyche.

MARIE-LOUISE VON FRANZ, *MAN AND HIS SYMBOLS*, EDITED BY C.G. JUNG (ALDUS BOOKS, 1964)

The four elements are the cornerstones of the Mysteries, to witches and initiates of many types. The symbolism of the number 4 is pervasive. It defines and stabilizes our earthly condition, being related to manifestation and completion. The four dimensions define our state, as length, breadth and width, and time, through which we move. The idea of four elements and four quarters is essential to the making of the magic circle, as indeed it is basic to psychic wholeness. Jung used the image of the mandala as a symbol for individuation, the process of the developing Self, becoming-that-which-one-is meant-to-be. The mandala is a circular shape, featuring within its design a pattern of four, or multiples thereof. A circle divided into four is one of the oldest and most powerful symbols, and has meanings on many levels. This is relevant psychologically and magically. The circle is an image of the psyche, soul or spirit, while the cross or square signifies the world of matter, and these are brought together in magical workings.

As with many such concepts, it may take a while to appreciate and to resonate with the meanings of the four elements. Here we have a way of bringing order to our ideas and to the cosmos, a thing of beauty and power. However, we need to be clear about the four elements and their associations, for we need to be able to evoke them as part of the construction of the magic circle. Here is also a fifth element, ether, which is a subtle essence that interpenetrates the physical and forms a kind of force field around physical objects; it is sometimes possible to see the etheric fields as a blue aura, rather like cigarette smoke, around people, animals and sometimes things. This is the force that is employed in magical workings. If we wish to 'place' ether as a fifth element in our circle, we can put it at the centre. The five-point star, or pentagram, symbolizes the four elements along with ether. Many witches work instinctively with ether (without realizing it sometimes). For the purposes of constructing our circle, we need to be able clearly to understand, visualize and call on the presence of the four elements. We also need to be aware of the associations, images and ambience of each of them.

THE ELEMENT OF EARTH

Earth is the most solid of the elements. Scientifically it relates to atoms which are in the solid state, which means they are vibrating at a lower rate. Earth is about solidity, the here-and-now, reality as we know it. It relates to physical sensations of touching, seeing, smelling, tasting and hearing, and it is the medium by which we ground our spells. Tools that relate to the element of Earth are the pentacle, and stone. Some traditions also associate the shield with Earth, for it gives us protection. Whenever we feel ourselves under threat of any kind, even if it is just the 'threat' of becoming confused or spaced out, we can use the Earth-invoking pentagram to bring us back to sense and safety. Some traditions use the Earth-invoking pentagram at all times because it is so basic and strong. It is formed

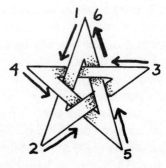

Earth-invoking pentagram

starting at the top apex and going down towards the left, as shown in the diagram. The pentagram is specially used to invoke the element of Earth. It is best to 'close off' your pentagram by a final stroke which goes once again over the path of your first stroke, reinforcing it.

Earth is associated with North, with death/rebirth, with Winter and with dark moon. We usually place our altar in the North of the circle, because the North is the 'blind side' of the sky, where Sun and Moon never travel, for witchcraft is a path of the hidden and the unconscious. When invoking the elements, Earth is first in line, because it is our source and our destiny, the womb and the tomb. It relates to our passage into and out of the manifest world, and to our own powers to do, and to actualize. In the North of the sky wheel are the circumpolar stars, known to the Celts as Caer Arianrhod. Arianrhod is goddess of the Silver Wheel, related to spider and weaver goddesses, and awesome mistress of birth, initiation, death and rebirth. Earth and North relate to practicality, groundedness, wisdom and truth. However, witches in the southern hemisphere will probably wish to rotate these associations through 180 degrees, as for you South is the 'blind side' of the sky, and thus your mysterious realm.

Each of the elements has its own type of spirits, and these are similar to the more general idea of nature spirits, or faeries. These are beings who are on a different evolutionary path from us, and who do not inhabit the physical world in the way that we do, but may be discerned on the fringes of it, when touched by Otherworld. We anthropomorphize these beings, seeing them as humanoid, but the truth is probably that they are energy and consciousness centres of a specific and powerful kind. There are different varieties of these spirits, some being more differentiated and 'intelligent' as we would normally use the term, while others are more instinctual. These entities have functions in the natural world, tending and protecting. They are real! They are led by a guiding spirit, a deva or 'elemental king'. The idea of 'elemental king' is an ancient one, possibly deriving from a tribal culture. In Wicca the four quarters are called the Watchtowers, and the leader of the relevant elementals is the Lord of the Watchtower. However, many witches prefer to think in other ways. Some witches simply visualize the elements as forces. I see the elemental devas as a Lady and a Lord, and I evoke them in that way, as 'Lady and Lord of the North ...' To me the Elemental Lady brings the elemental essence; she presides and oversees while the Elemental Lord provides the driving force. However you conceive the elements, they are beings of great power, and while they will consent to be summoned they must be treated with respect.

Folklore describes different sorts of 'faery folk' that may be encountered, and while again these may be subjective and very human images of spirits and forces that are non-human in nature, nonetheless they are meaningful to us. Earth spirits are called Gnomes, and from fairy tales we know that Gnomes are like little old men, who dwell deep within the earth. Gnomes tend the mineral deposits within the Earth, the crystals, precious stones and metals, ore, fossils, and sometimes they are jealous guardians. They also help with the fertility of the soul, and their activities may be associated with so-called 'ley lines'. Gnomes are often nearby when we are gardening, or close to the earth in any way.

The Greek name for the North wind, Boreas (pronounced 'Bo-rus'), is also used in Wiccan invocations.

Summary of Earth associations

North (probably South, in the southern hemisphere); midnight; midwinter; Yule; old age; Dark Moon; pentacle; stone; shield; Gnomes; Boreas; astrological signs – Taurus, Virgo, Capricorn; cold and dry; colours – black, brown (and some say yellow).

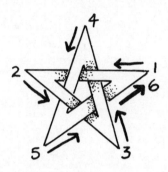

Air-invoking pentagram

THE ELEMENT OF AIR

The elements are invoked in turn, starting with the North and moving deosil around the circle. Deosil actually means 'in the direction of the Sun', so while this is clockwise in the northern hemisphere, in the southern it is anticlockwise. Air is associated with east, so moving clockwise from the North we come to Air next, while moving anticlockwise from the South, we also come to East at our next station.

The airy state is the most mobile, least dense state atoms may attain, while retaining stability. Gases are invisible. We discern the motion of the wind, not because we see it streak past, but because we see the trees bend and sway with its passage. Air is uncontainable, swift moving, elusive and energizing. It relates to thought, communication, travel, movement, inspiration and to the creative functioning of the mind which, like the wind, is visible only in its effects. In modern life it relates to such things as telephones and computers. Magically, the tool that carries the power of Air is the athame, and the censer and incense symbolises Air, also. Some traditions, namely Wicca, also use the sword, which is equated with Air. Air is linked to youth, dawn, Spring and waxing Moon.

The Air-invoking pentagram starts as the right apex, moving to the left point, then downwards, as shown on page 65. An easy way to remember this is to start with the point that is furthest from the altar, meaning our first stroke towards it. However, if you live in the southern hemisphere, and have your altar in the South, the reverse will apply. Many people feel that it is an unnecessary complication to form the pentagram in a variety of ways, and stick with the North/Earth-invoking pattern. This avoids the debate about whether it is symbolically correct to use the same formation as you used to invoke one element, to banish another, which we shall encounter shortly. It also avoids rethinking pentagrams for workings in the southern hemisphere, e.g. whether you should use the Earth-invoking pentagrams, even when placing Earth in the South, etc. Some people enjoy such debates, and no doubt to some they are important. To me they seem to stray from magic into the mind-games so beloved of the left brain, missing the point of witchcraft. When in doubt, keep it simple.

As we have seen, Air is associated with the East, where the sun rises and light is born, stretching its first eager fingers across the sky. The East is where all heavenly bodies rise. In astrology, the sign on the Eastern horizon describes our outward personality, our meeting with the world and our lens on life. It is fixed by the moment of birth, the entry into time and into separate existence, when our consciousness moves out of the maternal matrix to develop its independence. The element of Air is about this movement, this freshness, the excitement of discovery and of knowledge. The god that I associate especially with this element and direction is Mercury: winged messenger, patron of commerce, travel, communication, and protector of tricksters and magicians. Sometimes almost androgynous, at others depicted as a phallic Herm, Mercury/Hermes was the only god of the Graeco/Roman pantheon who could travel freely in and out of the Underworld, in the same way that our ability to reflect makes bridges between our conscious and unconscious minds.

The elemental spirits of Air are called the Sylphs. The Sylphs dance on mountain peaks, where the wind blows from horizon to horizon. They swoop playfully about tree-tops, and many trees are beloved of Sylphs because trees themselves have much in common with the element of Air. Sylphs cleanse the atmosphere and keep open the channels of communication, of all sorts. Wherever the air is fresh and the atmosphere free, you may be sure Sylphs are winging close by.

To invoke Air, Wiccans use the Greek name for the East wind, Eurius (pronounced 'Yoo-rus').

Summary of Air associations

East; dawn; Spring; Spring Equinox; youth; athame; sword; censer and incense; astrological signs – Gemini, Libra, Aquarius; Sylphs; hot and moist; colour – blue (possibly bright yellow).

THE ELEMENT OF FIRE

Fire is the most volatile of the elements. When something is on fire its molecules are in an excited state, changing from one substance to another. Fire leaps and dances, glows and smoulders, consumes and energizes. In human life Fire

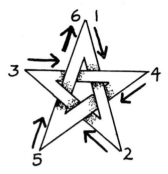

Fire-invoking pentagram

corresponds to visions and creativity, the big picture, drive, imagination, spirituality, ambition and inspiration. The inspirations of Fire are less the subtle associations spotted by Air, more a dynamic revelation. Air is the medium in which Fire flourishes. Thus our detached, untrammelled perspective can clear the way for some real brilliance. The tools magically associated with fire are the candle and the wand, although some traditions equate the wand with Air and the athame with Fire. For me, wands have sparks at the tip, as even Disney knows! And so the wand is a tool for the inspirational, while the athame favours concentration. This is, of course, up to you, as the practitioner, and you can make the choice that fits in best with your own outlook.

In the northern hemisphere, Fire is naturally associated with the South, where the sun shines and where the Full Moon glows. We link everything that is passionate, full-blooded and vital with the South. Fire/South represents all that draws us onwards and fires us with enthusiasm, strong feelings, wonderful ideas and a notion of the possible. It represents what we may become, our goals and aspirations that lift us out of the commonplace. For those of you who live in the southern hemisphere, however, this will be very different and it seems more fitting to equate Fire with North. The Fire-invoking pentagram starts at the top apex and moves down to the right this time, not to the left as for Earth.

Fire is linked to young adulthood, midday, Summer and the Summer Solstice. Goddesses of the hearth and sacred flame such as Vesta and Hestia may be associated with Fire, as well as the Irish sun goddess Grain, or Grainne, and Egyptian Sekhmet. Bride/Brighid too is a Fire goddess, and she is most vividly felt at Imbolc. The Olympic heavyweights Zeus/Jupiter, Mars/Ares and Apollo are associated with Fire and the Sun. Fire spirits are called Salamanders. We may spot these when we look for fire-pictures – something which is absent from modern homes that have no open fire. Salamanders leap and crackle in the flames of a bonfire, they shimmer in the heat of the Sun, and they are drawn to the candle flame, which they tend. The Greek name for the South wind is Notus.

Summary of Fire associations

South (in the northern hemisphere); midday; Summer; Summer Solstice; young adulthood; Full Moon; candle; wand; Salamanders; hot and dry; astrological signs – Aries, Leo, Sagittarius; colours – red and very bright orange.

THE ELEMENT OF WATER

Travelling clockwise around our circle we come to the direction West and the element of Water. If you are working in the southern hemisphere you will probably have travelled anticlockwise, now also arriving finally in the western quarter. Water is our final element, and in some ways the deepest. Atoms in a liquid state are fluid, but easily perceived and felt. You can hold water but you cannot keep it, feeling it soft and cool on your palms as it finds the cracks between your fingers and disappears. Water reflects experience and change, relating to the depths of the soul and its hidden currents, to feelings and body-wisdom, memory and tradition. Within us Water relates to empathy and compassion, love and healing, cleansing and evolving.

The tools linked to Water are the chalice and the cauldron. (Cauldron may also be associated with ether.) We all grew from a few tremulous cells into a fully-formed infant, within the amniotic 'cauldron' of the womb, so water is a creative element, but it is also an element of dissolution, as it slowly erodes substances as hard as granite. Water relates to all feelings and human bonds, but it also evokes the dissolving of these bonds as we come close to entering Otherworld, at death or during meditation. The Isles of the Blessed were situated in the West, the direction of Water. These are the eternal Summerlands, where souls may rest between incarnations. It is the element and the direction of peace.

In the British Isles it has always been natural to equate West with Water because we have the vast expanse of the Atlantic to the West, and rain blows in from the West. In other parts of the world, other directions may feel more appropriate for Water. In some North American traditions, for instance the Lakota, Water is equated with South. However, the association of West with Water runs deep in the blood of anyone with Anglo-Saxon or Celtic ancestry. In the West the Sun, Moon and all heavenly bodies set, going to their rest and to a place of peace. Water and West are linked to evening, Autumn and old age, which is the time we prepare for our final journey, out of our present incarnation. Goddesses such as Hecate may be linked to the West and to Water, for Water relates to the instinctual magic of the Feminine, and to the approach of darkness. Seductive female images such as the Melusine or Siren represent the allure of the watery, imaginal depths, which can promise secret delights, wonderful experience, but may actually overwhelm a fragile consciousness. The great Irish faery queen, Fand, lover of Mannannan of the sea, is a water goddess. She rules the Land-over-wave and flew as a seabird into our world, to entrap lovers such as the mighty hero Cuchulain. Water and Earth are usually considered to be feminine elements, while Fire and Air are thought of as masculine. Needless to say, they are both meaningful and accessible for both sexes.

Water may be invoked by tracing a pentagram, starting with the left-hand apex and moving horizontally to the right, as shown. Water spirits are called Undines, and they haunt all stretches of water, slipping into and out of the still waters with scarcely a ripple, singing in the waterfall and in the rhythm of the wave breaking in the strand, combing their long hair by the side of the stream. Sitting by the waterside, in moments of peace and mystical vision, you will catch sight of them out of the corner of your eyes. The name of the West wind is Zephyrus.

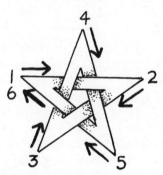

Water-invoking pentagram

Summary of Water associations

West; evening; Autumn; Autumn Equinox; middle of old age; waning Moon; chalice; cup; cauldron; Undines; astrological signs – Cancer, Scorpio, Pisces; cold and moist; colours – shades of green and sometimes purple; Zephyrus.

THE FOUR FUNCTIONS OF CONSCIOUSNESS

The four elements are very ancient indeed, possessing an archtypal significance. This means that they have a powerful ambience to which our unconscious resonates; they are mighty symbols that are instinctively meaningful to us and can lead us towards inner transformations. The term 'archtype' was used especially in this sort of context by the pioneer psychologist C.G. Jung, erstwhile pupil of Freud and founder of analytical psychology. In contrast to Freud, who concentrated upon the sexual drives, Jung found that the principle force within the human being was a spiritual one: the journey towards wholeness, individuation and realization of the Self. We have seen that the circle and the four elements are a type of mandala, which is a symbol for the complete and balanced Self. Jung also identified four functions of consciousness that correspond closely with the four elements and their attendant characteristics, and he taught that these all need to be developed and consciously functioning in order to attain individuation and spiritual wholeness. In this Jung reinterpreted some very ancient material, making it meaningful and acceptable in a modern context. However, the traditions upon which he drew were essentially magical ones.

The four functions of consciousness are thinking, feeling, sensation and intuition. This idea is being adapted and expanded by modern psychologists and used in psychological profiling, but the basics still hold good. The four functions correspond with Air, Water, Earth and Fire, respectively. Most people have one, or perhaps two functions consciously accessible. Sometimes a third may operate as auxiliary, but the great majority of us have one 'inferior' function, with which we cannot cope at any price and which operates as some sort of demon in our lives. Often our 'inferior' function may be identified most easily by what we can't do, for what we can do we take for granted. Thinking and feeling are evaluative while sensation and intuition are perceptual, and Jung taught that it is not possible to have both perceptual functions or both evaluative functions uppermost at the same time. Thus if intuition is your dominant mode, sensation is probably inferior; likewise if thinking is paramount, feeling will be inferior, and vice versa.

Any description of the four functions fails to catch the essence, for we can discern their manifestation only. Thus many intuitives will not regard themselves as using their intuition in any way, and by no means all of them are what we would term 'psychic'. Many intuitives are apparently practical, because they are often goal-orientated. However, intuition takes in the whole picture, instinctively picking out the important points and the essential meanings, spotting things that are peripheral in one sense but may be vital in another. What the intuitive sees is greater than the sum of its parts. Intuitives certainly may follow hunches, sometimes have an essentially playful approach, projecting consciousness outwards, into their surroundings, into the future, concerned with what may be possible, sowing seeds of inspiration but not always staying to reap. If you are an intuitive then sensation is probably your weakest function. Car and kitchen may be filled with gremlins and the lock on your own front door may be more puzzling than Schrodinger's cat.

Sensation function is the 'reality function'. Someone whose sensation function is highly developed copes well with the material world and is rooted in the evidence of the five senses. Sensation types often notice details and aren't fazed by practical problems. Often they seem very logical, but this isn't a theoretical logic but rather the logic of what works. Sensation people are not fascinated by what may be, but focus on what is. If you are a sensation type your intuition may be least well-developed, and so you may be deeply suspicious of the fantastical. Speculation may make you uneasy, imagination is tricky and anything smacking of spirituality highly suspect. Sensation types and intuitives are often drawn together because each can do what the other can't, and while there are always difficulties when differences are extreme, these two may happily inhabit parallel universes, as long as there is mutual respect. Sensation looks on indulgent and fascinated, as intuition pursues all these wild schemes, while intuition is mesmerized by the matter of fact way sensation changes a plug (but in the worst scenario intuition feels suffocated and misunderstood, while sensation feels threatened). Where there is a reasonable degree of psychic health we tend to admire and seek our 'inferior' function, thus the intuitive may like to do cooking or woodwork and the sensation type may be drawn to science fiction.

Thinking and feeling are also two pairs of opposites. It is important to understand that Jung regarded feeling as a rational function. This had all the professors (who were probably thinking types) jumping about, because feeling is regarded as just the opposite in our culture, where control and logic are regarded as the summit of human achievement. Thinking and sensation are valued over intuition and feeling in our Western society. However, feeling is indeed rational, weighing things in terms of human value, human bonds. Feeling types understand the human being and relationships, traditions, family bonds. Feeling is not the same as emotion in this sense, although the feeling-type may process emotions more smoothly. To the feeling type, beauty is truth. If you are a feeling type you will readily understand that feeling is different from emotion. In addition you will probably be in tune with the prevailing mores of society. It will be hard for you to think in a logical, detached fashion, and when you are asked what you think, you will probably say what you feel, for you will assess human value, not logical structure. When pressed to give your opinions they may come out as a bit half-baked and surprisingly rigid. You regard too much analysis as cold and irrelevant.

If you are a thinking type, to you truth is beauty, and you like people to say what they think, and to mean what they say. Emotions are all very well, and we know they have a place, but they should be kept in it. You are able to be detached, travelling from one idea to the other, looking at its merits in a dispassionate manner. You are likely to be clever, and the higher echelons of academia are thronged with thinking types. However, no function has the monopoly on intelligence, and there are plenty of doctors who have feeling paramount. Although thinking types are often aware of having powerful emotions, they may deny them or keep them repressed (not the same as reasonable control, although few thinking types quite appreciate this). Thinking types fear being overwhelmed by emotion, may have trouble saying what they like and expressing how they feel, and may be inconveniently ambushed by feelings such as falling in love with the 'wrong' person. Thinking and feeling are often drawn together, and this doesn't always make for an easy relationship because each sees the world very differently. Feeling is hurt by the seeming lack of warmth, response and concern of the thinking type, and thinking can't understand why feeling is so disturbingly 'irrational' and out of control. However, our opposites have much to offer us, which is why we are attracted to them.

In the same way that the four elements/quarters are marked out on the magic circle, so the human psyche can be shown as a sphere divided into four, as in the diagram overleaf. Whichever function is opposite, the superior function will be 'inferior' and unconscious, so we can show the sphere divided into conscious and unconscious. Of course, because a function is unconscious in us this does not mean we do not have it – we do, and it will certainly operate within us, but unconsciously. Thus, for instance, the unconscious feeling of the thinking type may take her or him over in inconvenient passions that arise seemingly from nowhere (and history shows that 'rational' scientists are often driven by unacknowledged prejudice and desire). When we begin to consider the unconscious we move into highly complex territory. Suffice to say that we all strive for balance and to access our inferior function. This is an enormous undertaking, for a fully differentiated individual is a rarity.

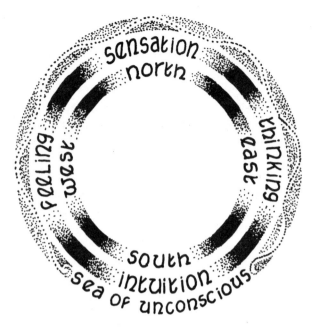

The four functions of consciousness

Do not believe anyone who says they have attained it, especially if they are under forty! Someone who is approaching this is a person of considerable presence. Simply recognizing these differences and accepting them, however, is a great step forward, and it can be very helpful in our relationships when we truly register that the other person is coming from somewhere completely different. It can also show us the way to further growth. Quite possibly you can recognize your superior functions from the above descriptions, and from what you find most alien to you, and often the functions that you simply 'like best' are the ones you have paramount.

Each of the four functions corresponds to one of the elements: intuition and Fire; feeling and Water; thinking and Air; sensation and Earth. The zodiacal sign under which we were born may be a clue to our dominant function.

When we form our magic circle we are creating a sphere of wholeness and our unconscious recognizes that fact. Thus making the circle is an important exercise on a psychological level. More than this, when we invoke the element that corresponds to our weakest function we are helping strengthen and develop that function. One clue of your 'inferior' function may appear as the element that you find most difficult to invoke. Even if your concentration is total and your visualization vivid, something in you will probably resonate especially to your principle element/function, while that corresponding to your inferior function may seem more elusive, and perhaps more awesome. So making the circle is in itself part of our inward journey. When we form our magic circle we are, at some level, creating an environment where we can become whole.

Magic circle showing correspondences

INVOKING THE ELEMENTS

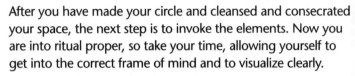

After you have made your circle and cleansed and consecrated your space, the next step is to invoke the elements. Now you are into ritual proper, so take your time, allowing yourself to get into the correct frame of mind and to visualize clearly.

When you are ready, face your altar, which will be in the North of your circle, or if you are in the southern hemisphere, you will probably have chosen to place your altar in the South. Whichever, the first element to be invoked is the element of Earth. Start to feel the presence of Earth, the deep breath of the mountains, the secrecy of caves, the scent of the soils as new rain falls. Say something on the lines of the following:

> *Lady and Lord of the North, O powers of Earth*
> *Be with me now, guard my circle and my rites*
> *Ground my deeds and make them fertile*
> *By hill and dale, deep cave, old bone*
> *By fertile field and soil and stone*
> *Be here now, ye powers of Earth.*

Draw the Earth-invoking pentagram in the air with your athame or fingertip, seeing a stream of blue light emanating from it. Now see the shape of the pentagram you have drawn, flaming in the air about your circle. Visualize elemental Earth entering into your sacred space through the centre of the pentagram. The coming of the elements is awesome. It may even bring tears to your eyes. However, if nothing dramatic is felt, don't worry. Bow, with your arms crossed over your chest, and your fingertips at your shoulders (the Osiris risen position, called 'standing as witches'). Say, 'Welcome, my Lady, my Lord of Earth,' and turn deosil to the East.

Now is the turn of Air. Begin to feel the rush of the wind, as if you were on a mountaintop. Fix your inward eye on a far horizon. The sky is blue and brilliant, all is freedom, freshness and scintillating energy. Say these words:

> *Lady and Lord of the East, O powers of Air*
> *Be with me now, guard my circle and my rites*
> *Give wings to my thoughts, clear my vision*
> *By wind and cloud, tall mountain's height*
> *By blue horizon, morning light*
> *Be here now, ye powers of Air.*

Draw the Air-invoking pentagram (or simply repeat the Earth-invoking pentagram, which is the 'basic'). Feel and visualize the entrance of elemental Air. Bow and say 'Welcome'. Turn deosil to the South.

Here you are invoking Fire. Now you will see huge leaping flames that crackle and rush, but do not consume. Fireworks explode, bright as the midday Sun. You are gazing into the heart of pure energy. Say these words:

> *Lady and Lord of the South, O powers of Fire*
> *Be with me now, guard my circle and my rites*
> *Inspire me, fill me with energy*
> *Bonfire, beacon, burning bright*
> *Embers rich, wild lightning strike*
> *Be here now, ye powers of Fire.*

Draw the Fire-invoking pentagram (or again, simply the Earth pentagram). Feel and see the entrance of elemental Fire. Bow and bid 'Welcome'. Turn deosil to the West.

Now you will invoke the element of Water. Allow peace to come upon you, stillness to ripple through you. Before you lies a deep green lake, into which slowly drops a waterfall. Silver droplets fall upon your face and the cool scent of the water is all about you. Say these words:

> *Lady and Lord of the West, O powers of Water*
> *Be with me now, guard my circle and my rites*
> *Bring me your healing and your wisdom*

> *Green-hearted lake and river wide*
> *Crystal fountain, ocean tide*
> *Be here now, ye powers of Water.*

Bow and bid welcome as before. Turn finally to your altar and stand quietly for a moment. Now your circle is complete and your rites may begin. (When setting up your circle, you don't need a compass, just a rough idea of the directions will suffice.)

WICCAN APPROACH

Wiccans have specific ways of invoking the elements which are summoned, rather than asked to be present (my preferred method), but I don't think the elemental monarchs mind, as long as there is an atmosphere of respect. Usually the High Priest invokes them, and the pentagram is formed differently for each element. The words are:

> *Ye Lords of the Watchtowers of the North, Boreas, ye*
> *Lords of Earth. I do summon, I do stir and I do call thee*
> *up, to guard this circle and to witness these rites …*

With the words 'I do summon …' the High Priest begins to form the pentagram with his athame, completing it by the word 'rites'. Now he stabs the centre of the pentagram with his athame as the elemental powers enter on a word of power, drawn from the Qabbalah. The High Priest says, 'Hail, Boreas' and this is echoed by the rest of the coven. Not all covens use quite the same method, and sometimes Celtic names may be used, or no name at all.

The Wiccan approach is more dramatic and compelling. When we do magic it is important that we are able to assume an attitude of command. Whether you feel that this is the correct approach here, or not, depends on you.

BANISHING/FAREWELL

When all ritual is complete the final action is to 'banish' the elemental powers. Again, personally I do not like the idea of banishing these forces, but rather of thanking them, bidding them farewell and closing the portals to Otherworld. It is important that this closure is properly effected, so devote some concentration to this. Turn first to the North (South, if you wish, in the southern hemisphere) and say:

> *Lady and Lord of the …, thank you for being present at my rites. Until we meet again, may you return to the glory of your world. I now bid you Hail and Farewell.*

Imagine the door to Otherworld closing, like a great eye. Travel deosil around your circle, closing down each of the directions/elements in turn. Some traditions close down 'widdershins', which is the opposite direction to deosil, starting in the West and moving anticlockwise (in the northern hemisphere). This makes perfect sense, because widdershins is about undoing and banishing, but there are those who avoid widdershins working, believing it to hold something nasty. I feel this hardly makes sense. It is something you may like to think about.

You may form the basic Earth-invoking pentagram each time, or use banishing pentagrams. North/Earth banishing starts at the left base apex and moves upwards, East starts at the left and moves right, South starts at the base right and moves upwards, West starts at the right and moves left. (The Earth-banishing pentagram may also be used during pathworking, as a protection on inward journeys from anything unpleasant that you may encounter.) Wiccans start banishing in the East and use these words:

> *Ye Lords of the Watchtowers of the East, Eurious, ye Lords of Air, we thank you for attending our rites and ere ye depart to your pleasant and lovely realms, we bid you hail and farewell.*

You may visualize the energy you have put into invoking the elements now being drawn back inside, via the point of your athame, if you are using one. It is important to pull all this back and to close everything down, or you may feel spaced out and your energies will be left around your circle. Breathing in may help, although witches do this instinctively. Concentrate on this, but do not agonize. If you affirm that you are closing down, drawing in, turning off, then the chances are that you are succeeding.

Choices   In this chapter there have been several choices to make regarding the elements, how you visualize them, how you invoke them, even what tools you use and what directions you associate with each element. These choices are yours to make, if you are working alone, but if you are training in a specific tradition you will naturally need to follow your trainer or High Priestess or Priest. If you are working alone, do think carefully about these choices and give yourself time to arrive at something that feels right for you. Don't be in a hurry to arrive at a decision, if you feel unsure. Give yourself time to meditate. Finally, be clear, don't chop and change in the middle of a ritual. It is important to remember that, while witchcraft is a tradition, not a dogma, traditions are often based on deep meaning and should not be lightly discarded.

Practice   One of the most important bits of magical 'routine' is your pentagram formation. Pentagrams are useful in many type of ritual, as protection and invocation. Get used to visualizing them, forming them in the air, and drawing endless pentagrams on paper. Again there is a choice, whether you will stick with the basic pentagram, or use different pentagrams for different purposes. Think about what feels right, and make up your mind. Of course, you may change your mind at some point, but that is different from adopting one course one day, changing to another the next.

Closeness to the elements   Many witches identify the elements instinctively, and it is probable that the entire idea is second nature to you. However, this may not be the case, for logical thinking processes often overlay intuition. Whatever the case, practise never comes amiss, so you may like to do some simple exercises, to train your perceptions. One exercise is to list all the words you associate with each element on a sheet of paper, drawing what comes to mind if you like, or making a collage. So for Water you might list words such as peaceful, feeling, healing, gentle, powerful, deep, mermaid, seal, whale etc. You might decorate your page with greens, bluey-greens, purples, with drawings of fish, waves, bits of shiny paper to indicate water etc. Another exercise is to go out into your locality and gather natural substances that symbolize the elements. You may like to do this walking in the direction associated with the element. As an example the sort of things you might gather on a beach could be:

> **Earth** – black or dark brown pebble, sample of sand, fish skeleton
> **Air** – feather, blue pebble, pointed stone
> **Water** – green pebble, shell, sample of seawater, seaweed
> **Fire** – red pebble, combustible driftwood, wand-shaped wood

There are many other things you might find, some human-made and some natural. Walk out and look, in a playful mood, and see what you find.

Elemental pathworking   We shall be looking at pathworking in a later chapter. A pathworking to meet the elements is a vivid way of getting to know them.

5

MAGICAL TOOLS
AND SYMBOLS

> *Cords and censer, scourge and knife*
> *Powers of the witches' blade*
> *Waken all ye unto life,*
> *Come ye as the charm is made.*

DOREEN VALIENTE, THE WITCHES RUNE

THE IMPORTANCE OF TOOLS

Tools and artefacts are important in magic because they have the important property of focusing the conscious mind through their effect on the unconscious. Tools have a symbology, some of which is obvious, some less so, but either way this symbolic language is heard loud and clear by the unconscious, which then contributes its enormous power to the undertaking. There is a tradition behind the use of the tools of witchcraft which is enshrined in our race memory, and so gives them power. The setting out of magical tools is a ritual in itself, which is saying to the unconscious, 'time to get going!' and so this forms part of the shift in consciousness, the move into stillness that draws us close to Otherworld. In addition, magical tools become infused with the energy of their owner, and come replete with old associations of other rites and spells. (I have used the terms 'subconscious' and 'unconscious' almost interchangeably in this paragraph. Strictly speaking the subconscious is generally below the level of ordinary consciousness, but may be accessed fairly readily in the right circumstances, whereas the unconscious is deeper and partakes of that vast seas of consciousness that connects us with the whole of our race, which Jung called the 'collective unconscious'. Both levels are important in the intuitive realm of magic.)

Having said this, there are two other elements to be born in mind. One is that sometimes spells and rituals may be effected without any props at all, and there are people who have experienced success in this way, including myself. If your imagination is powerful, props can occasionally be a distraction. Another point, very much in contrast to this, is that I believe it can be a mistake to dismiss magical tools as 'just symbolic', merely possessing the property of mobilizing the human mind, having no inherent power of their own, for this de-mythologizes the material world in a way that isn't consistent with the approach of the witch. Even if you do not always use your tools, they are an anchor. If your intuitive faculty (as described in the previous chapter) is paramount, as it is with many witches, then tools help you to connect with your sensation function. If sensation is strong in you, then the symbolism of tools, which will resonate within your unconscious, helps you to access your intuition. Either way, the tools of the witch are things of beauty and a sort of 'badge of office'. They are a concrete statement of your path, as witch and priestess or priest.

THE PRINCIPLE TOOLS

Athame

The athame (pronounced 'ath-AY-me') is a ritual knife. It is from this description that some of the more lurid accounts of the activities of witches may well have arisen! However, the athame is quite explicitly never ever used to cut anything in the material world. The athame symbolizes the cutting edge of the intellect, not used to shred and demolish, but to differentiate and direct. With the point of your athame you focus your intent and fix your concentration, using it to direct power. The athame says, 'Upon this do I bend my entire will'. The athame also 'cuts reality', creating portals to Otherworld. The athame, as we have seen, is connected to the element of Air. However, some say that this is a later, and misleading, amendment to an older tradition linking the athame with Fire, and this would correlate with the stream of energy that we send through the tip of the athame. Nonetheless, the athame, for me, connects with Airas, the medium of the lightning-flash. In the end, it is up to you how you perceive it.

Wand

Magical practitioners do have wands, and this is related to the element of Fire. The ancients believed that Fire lay dormant within wood, waiting to leap into life as real flame. Both wand and athame can be seen as phallic, and thus related to the male principle, to going forth rather than being and containing, and sometimes you may feel they are interchangeable. I think that it is no accident that wands in children's storybooks are depicted with sparks at the tip, and I do feel that the wand relates to Fire, rather than to Air, as some traditions indicate. Thus I would use a wand in rituals connected to the properties of elemental Fire. My feeling is that the athame is for directing and focusing my own energies, while the wand is for entering the realm of energies already present and working with them, such as when working with the energies of the Full Moon, when I would usually use a willow wand. Of course, you can function without a wand, if you wish. As you become used to your tools you will get a feeling of how they wish to be employed.

Your wand can be obtained in several ways. Firstly you may select a tree and ask it if you may take one of its small branches as your wand. It may be best to 'get to know' your tree first, by visiting and communing, which may sound odd behaviour to some but is a very real way of drawing close to the natural world. If you ask your tree, you must be aware of the answer, although this is unlikely to be 'no' if you have harmonized with the tree. Another way is simply to walk into a wood, going where your nose leads you, and see where you are led, which tree you find yourself before. If you cut a wand, be sure to do it sensibly, leaving the tree tidy, and thank the tree for supplying it to you. Rub your left thumb over the 'wound' as a healing gesture for the tree. Alternatively, you may just use fallen wood for your wand. Finally, fine wands can be bought, with jewels at the tip and carvings upon them. You can fix precious stones, or an acorn or cone, on a wand that you make, and carve symbols on it. It is best to oil your new wand with grapeseed oil, or another vegetable oil, to keep it supple.

Wands made from different woods are said to carry specific properties. Hazel wands were reputedly used by the Celts, as hazel has mercurial characteristics, carrying with it blinding flashes of insight. The Gaelic white wand was of yew, very slow-growing and related to the wisdom of the Goddess. Rowan wands are protective, and rowan trees are said to stand, as guardians of the energies of the Earth, on ley lines. The wand of Merlin was made of oak, a commanding and powerful tree; ash unites male and female and relates to far-flung communication and the forces that underpin Nature. For the Norse, the World Tree was Yggdrasil, or the ash. Willow is connected to water and the Moon. Whatever wood it is made from, the wand is a living connection to the timeless world of trees.

Chalice

Take time to choose your chalice, for it will be a loving companion during rituals, holding pure water or fragrant wine, and bringing with it the blessing of the Goddess.

Related to the element of Water, the chalice is essential in most rituals, and you can use it to hold wine for consecration. The symbolism of the chalice is powerful, relating to all the old legends about the Holy Grail, where the hero seeks the wisdom of the Feminine. The chalice represents the ability of the female to contain and to nurture, and it has obvious links with the womb. This is a working accoutrement, so your chalice should not be too delicate. Pottery or pewter chalices may be best, with a short stem and a broad base.

Pentacle

Much has been said about the pentagram, or five-point star, as an important constituent of ritual. The pentagram is a very potent magical sign, having several meanings. It is the body of woman, whereas the six-point star may be seen as a man's body; it is the four elements along with the fifth element of ether; it is the creative mind at work with the four elements, and it also has links with the pattern of the orbit of Venus. It has geometric connections with the proportion of the Golden Section, which refers to the division of a line or rectangle in such a way that the smaller portion is in relation to the larger, in the same way that the larger relates to the whole. This is a most pleasing proportion, found throughout nature and underlying many ancient structures, from stone circles to Gothic cathedrals. The pentagram is a symbol with immense resonance, whose mysteries we cannot totally plumb.

The terms 'pentacle' and 'pentagram' are often used interchangeably. Strictly speaking the pentacle is a disk upon which the pentagram or five-point star is inscribed. The pentacle is a vital part of ritual, placed on the altar to symbolize the element of Earth. Pentacles can be made out of metal or wood.

Candle

Candles are basic to ritual and indeed a potent ritual can be concocted from a candle, and nothing else. Obviously linked to the element of Fire, the candle flame is a sign of illumination and transformation. Candles may be placed at each of the four quarters and on the altar, and used as specific elements in ritual.

Censer

Incense is related to the element of Air. Incense isn't really a magical tool in the way that the wand or athame may be, although incense smoke may be specifically used in cleaning or consecrating. However, incense is vital in ritual, because scent speaks directly, through the primitive, reptilian brain-stem, to the unconscious. For your incense you may use a simple joss-stick. However, if you are serious about your rituals it is far better to have a supply of different raw incenses to burn on charcoal.

You may burn incense in any thick container, but do be careful because this may become very hot indeed. An ashtray won't do: you need something stronger. It is preferable to have a censer, because you can lift this and waft it over your area. Charcoal may need practice, but if it is kept in a dry place and tongs are used to hold it, you should get the hang of it. You can make you own incense from dried herbs bought in a supermarket, but again it is better to obtain your supplies from specialists (suppliers listed at the back of the book). In addition, herbs often smell unpleasant, and while the object of incense isn't just to smell nice (banishing incenses, for instance, may be very pungent), fragrance can have a positive effect on the spirit. For this, resins, such as majestic frankincense and warm copal, are worth investing in. Many New Age suppliers also stock ready-made recipes, named after gods and goddesses or festivals, but it is best to make your own, even if these are simple combinations. Using plant materials that you gather in the wild, or that you have grown yourself, is very special. Incense is covered in *Herbs for Magic and Ritual: A Beginner's Guide* (see Further Reading). A good basic incense can be made from frankincense, myrrh and cinnamon. The practice of using smudge sticks as incense is growing; this is a bundle of herbs such as sage and sweet-grass, which can be ignited, left to smoulder and wafted around the sacred area or through the aura. This derives more from Native American culture, and while it may be simpler, especially for outdoor rites, generally I prefer sprinkling incense on charcoal.

Cauldron

The cauldron is associated with the popular image of the witch. It relates to the element of water, but because of its very transformative associations, it may also be connected to ether. The cauldron represents the womb that is also the tomb, the passage into and out of the manifest world and the process of change, rebirth, reincarnation. The cauldron has links with the Goddess in Her darker aspect. Specifically it is linked to Cerridwen, who brewed a magic potion in her cauldron, drops of which spilt onto the wrong person, namely Gwion, who then acquired the magic powers of the brew. Cerridwen ate him, later giving birth to the bard Taliesin. So the cauldron symbolizes all our changes, our reforging in the cauldron of life, our revelations drawn from the depths, our creativity and our dissolution in the water of eternity. The cauldron is central to many rituals that honour the process of change in some form. Cauldrons may have four feet, relating thus to the four elements, or three, relating to the Triple Goddess. Some are cast-iron, or you may find a beautiful cauldron of copper. A large bowl may be used, instead, and some natural substances lend themselves to wonderful cauldron shapes.

Stone

Many witches like to place a special stone, or stones, upon their altar as an honour to the powers of Earth. Stones are especially sacred to the Goddess as transferring Her power. A suitable stone might actually be used in place of a pentacle.

White-handled knife

This is an actual working knife, used to cut herbs or scrape away at incense. Some traditions do not have a white-handled knife, but a black-handled knife, used for the same purposes. In actual fact, scissors or a penknife may serve you better.

Besom

Replete with symbolism, real witches indeed use the besom to sweep out and cleanse the circle, prior to ritual. Besoms are traditionally made from a variety of combination, the oldest being made from the broom plant, *Planta genista*. Other trees were used later, all having their own symbolism, some of which we have encountered in the section on the wand. Birch was a favourite, for the birch tree is linked to purification. More data on this can be found in *The Magic and Mystery of Trees* (see Further Reading). The witches broom is, of course, a proper besom, not an angular modern broom, and (please!) certainly not made from nylon and plastic. The penetration of the phallic handle into the feminine brush signifies the union of the sexes and fertility, both literal and metaphoric. Brooms were 'ridden' over the fields to ensure a good crop. The idea of flying on a broom probably originated in shamanic journeys, where the experience of spirit flight is central. Sexual ecstasy may be akin to out-of-body experience, and sex, as we know, is considered a powerful force by witches. Drugs may have been taken, and the handle of the broomstick could have been smeared with special ointments, to apply to the delicate vaginal tissue – the so-called flying ointment. The broomstick is still used in handfastings, or witch weddings, where the couple jump the broomstick as a sign of their altered state.

Book of Shadows

This is a notebook, preferably quite a large one, in which you make notes about your magical rites and the things that you have learned. Notes about rituals can be inscribed in this book prior to starting. This aids the memory and is a suitable reference when you may not want to be taking ordinary books into your circle. The Book of Shadows is so called because what is written can only be a 'shadow' of the mystical truth underlying it. Furthermore, it is a secret book – you will not want people dipping into your personal Book of Shadows. The coven Book of Shadows, which contains Wiccan mythology, rites, symbolism etc., is copied down by initiates as part of their training. Some people prefer the term Book of Illumination.

Sword

This is used by Wiccans at specific times, and has a symbolism akin to that of the athame. As the High Priestess wields it she shows that while men may wield the greatest physical power, on the spiritual planes it is the Feminine which is most powerful. Many traditions do not include any use of the sword. You may like it as a dramatic, medieval touch. Obviously the sword is phallic, but some men do not like the idea of their penis being weapon-like, and prefer the use of a staff as more natural, made of a warmer substance.

Scourge

Again, this belongs to Wiccan tradition. The scourge is symbolic of the ills of earthly life and shows how we have to submit to some bitter interludes and suffering if we are to change and progress, or even simply to live. In the Wiccan Legend of the Goddess, She consents to be scourged by the God, as Death, and is thus awakened to love. This symbolism is not intended to debase the Feminine in any way, but might be considered unfortunate by some, bearing in mind the historical position of women, and it does not seem to reflect fully the power of the Goddess to many witches. The scourge is used as part of Wiccan rites, but Wiccans aren't sadists and masochists! The scourge doesn't hurt at all, and is merely symbolic.

Cords

Some cord symbolism is quite complex and cords of different colours are used to mean different things. The basic witches' cord was used to measure out the circle, being $4^1/_2$ feet long, therefore measuring a circle of 9 feet in diameter, or 3 yards. The yard relates to megalithic culture and isn't an arbitrary measurement, so even if you choose not to have your circle this size, don't unthinkingly substitute metres, for they aren't the same. Cords may be used as symbolic binding, prior to initiation (but this should only be symbolic – you don't want to be tied to a chair if the house catches fire). Wiccans wear cords in a circle around the waist: red for women, blue for men. Cords can also be used in specific spells that require their imagery of binding and fixing.

Effigies

When you set out your altar it is very desirable to have an effigy of the Goddess, and one of the God. These may be statues, special stones or anything that appeals to you. Pictures may also be used.

Salt and water

You will need these in your rites, to purify your circle and to represent the elements of Water and Earth. The salt may be thought of as purifying the water. Sacred to Aphrodite, salt was a valuable substance to the ancients, for preserving and purifying. A salt bath can be taken before rites to prepare oneself, and salt is good for healing injuries.

Bell

This is useful to have in rituals. Its ringing can be symbolic, and the number of times it is rung can have meaning. It defines beginnings and endings and claims attention, releasing potent vibrations. It is symbolic of the Goddess, being bowl-shaped. Sound has a very magical significance and there are some disciplines where the resonance of words of power is of great importance. Indeed, there is evidence to suggest that the pyramids may have been built through the power of sound, which is a vibration. Most witches do not make much of this, and this may be because down the ages we learned to be quiet, in order to be safe. Lone witches often whisper their rites. However, the power of sound is worth reflection.

Whistle

Complementary to the bell is the penny-whistle, or, better still, Pan-pipes, with obvious God-symbolism. If someone can play this the ambience of the ritual can be tremendously enhanced. Other musical instruments, such as drums, may also be used.

Speculum

This is an article used for scrying, such as a crystal, black mirror or bowl of water. Scrying is the art of looking for images in such objects that are meaningful and/or prophetic. The images may be literally 'seen' or perceived with the mind's eye. Samhain is the traditional festival for this practice, and such objects are sacred to the Goddess.

Robe

Many witches' work is performed 'sky-clad', which means naked. However, some people do not like this. Certainly there are pros and cons. Nakedness honours the human body in the true spirit of the Craft. We are all equal when naked. Furthermore, some say that the subtle energies emanated by the body flow more freely when there are no clothes. Others say that if these energies are so weak as to be bothered by a bit of cloth then they can't amount to much, and that naked working is uncomfortable and asking for trouble in a mixed-sex coven. All these views have a place, and again it is up to you. Cold is often not felt in circle, but may be an issue! While the body may adapt amazingly well to nude working, even outside on a fairly chilly evening, when the air feels wonderful on bare skin, there are times when it is not practical, and I am sure our forbears usually used cloaks for reasons of concealment if nothing else. These choices depend on time, place and personality. Whatever the case, it is good to have a special robe for use at those times when nude working cannot be possible (such as when blessing a friend's house). It is best to have a robe that is kept for such situations alone, so it becomes charged with magical association. Such a robe may be made from some suitable fabric, in a dark colour of your choice (black is probably the most traditional, but some feel it's a witchcraft cliché, and prefer dark brown) and caught at the waist with a cord. Such a robe can be easily made with two strips of cloth the length of the body sewn together, but left open at the hem and neck. No hemming will be necessary if you choose a cloth that doesn't fray. If your strip of cloth is wide enough you can include sleeves, with little extra sewing. It is also good to have a special piece of jewellery that you only wear for rituals and some priestesses wear necklaces of amber and jet. Again you may choose whatever seems most compatible with your personal energies.

Other articles

Naturally you will need to have with you, in your circle, any materials you need for the spells you intend to perform, and seasonal decorations will be placed on the altar, for festivals, such as fruit, nuts, flowers and foliage.

Altar

Last, but not least, you will need some sort of an altar on which to place many of your ritual implements. This can be anything from a fine table down to a cardboard box, covered with a cloth. Ensure you set out your altar with love and care. The altar is placed in your circle to the North, although, as we have seen, those of you working as witches in the southern hemisphere will probably prefer to have the altar in the South. The altar is a devotional space, a working base and a shrine.

IMPORTANT SYMBOLS

We have already encountered several important symbols in the shape of the pentagram, the circle and the cross. The *pentagram*, shown with an apex pointing downwards, looks

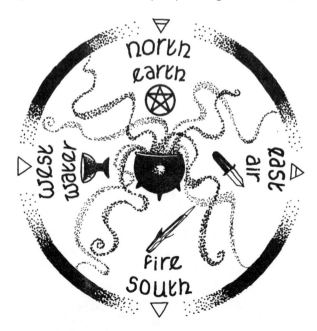

Important symbols

like a goat's head, and was considered a mark of evil. However, a better interpretation may be that it shows the creative mind at work within the earthly world. The *circle*, being the most perfect of shapes, has no end and therefore connects us with infinity. It is within the circle (or sphere) that magical rites take place. The *circle* also echoes the containing shape of the womb and our place here on Earth, with the sky wheeling around us. The *cross* is connected to the four elements, and the quartered circle signifies the four elements also. This can be seen in the Celtic Cross, and is also echoed in the Maltese Cross. The image of the equal-armed cross is much older than Christianity.

For your rites you may not need to know any more symbols, and some traditions use more complex symbolism than others. The closer we draw to ritual magic the more convoluted becomes the symbolism, whereas Nature magic keeps it simple. Here is a selection of symbols that you will find useful.

Ankh

This is a looped cross, and is especially associated with ancient Egypt, and some say with the menstrual napkin of the Goddess Isis. It symbolizes life, the upper loop linking to the Feminine with the downward stem connecting the Masculine. The shape of a key is also suggested, and the ankh may be key to the mysteries.

Triangle

The meaning of the number 3, in number symbolism, is creativity, and also relates to the Triple Goddess, or any grouping of three deities, which is very common in mythologies. Triangles are used by ritual magicians, placed outside the circle, to conjure demons. A triangle with the apex pointing down, like a chalice, signifies Woman, and pointing upwards, like a flame, signifies Man. These triangles may also mean Water and Fire, respectively. Air is similar to

Fire, but has another line inside, drawn parallel to the base. Earth resembles Water, but with another line inside, again drawn parallel to the base. Ether may be shown as a circle divided into six.

Six-point star

This signifies the male body, as the five-point star signifies the female. It is also the union of the triangles of Water and Fire, Feminine and Masculine, and so symbolizes balance. It is an ancient symbol, also called the Seal of Solomon, for Solomon was believed to have possessed a ring on which was engraved this symbol along with Tetragrammaton, or name of God, enabling him to control spirits. Thus this symbol is related to the control of spirits and because of the Fire/Water combination, the Philosopher's Stone of alchemy. It isn't routinely used in witchcraft.

The spiral

The spiral signifies movement into and out of the manifest world and also conveys the idea of cycle, such as that of the seasons, which is ever recurring, yet always different. The spiral is similar to the *labyrinth* as it means entrance to the Mysteries, where the eternal meets the here and now, where life meets death. In Greek myth the hero Theseus, helped by the weaving goddess, Ariadne, confronts the monsters of the unconscious as portrayed by the Minotaur, and emerges strong and victorious, having received his initiation. Ariadne gives the hero a thread, which relates to the cosmic web, or *net*, and the symbolism of this extends to the *knot*, worn by Cretan priestesses. When we become initiates we, too, enter the labyrinth and only the Goddess, who spins the thread of life, may show us the way out. This may also be linked to snakes, creatures symbolic of wisdom, which move in a spiralling fashion, and also to water as it spirals down a drain.

YOUR TOOLS

Part of becoming a witch is the collection of your own tools, and this can be fun, but also awesome. If often seems as if the right tool just comes to you, almost as a confirmation of what you need and the rightness of your path. Traditionally, the belief is that tools are best if made by the magical practitioner, and I am sure this is so, but not very practical in many cases! You can buy your tools, and it is a good idea to look in junk and bric-a-brac shops where magical objects may be found hiding. Of course, you can also buy your items new. Tradition teaches that we should never haggle over the price of any magical item. If you buy something that is old, cleanse it before using it, by leaving it in salt water for several hours. The running water of a stream will also operate as a cleanser. Having cleansed your object, it can be a good idea to leave it out in the light of the Full Moon, to 'charge it up'. Follow this with the ritual consecration, given in the following training session.

Store your magical equipment somewhere special, where it won't come into contact with day-to-day objects. I prefer to keep ritual objects separate, so they retain their specialness and don't become contaminated by the 'vibes' of other bits and bobs. However, not everyone agrees with this approach, because of course the witches of old were often very poor and would not have been able to afford special things, but would have used the tools from their own kitchens. Indeed, this affirms the sacredness of everyday life. There is good basis for turning simple jobs, such as kneading bread-dough, into a ritual or spell in itself. Besides this, there may not always be time to get out the full regalia from your 'magic box' and to allow yourself to be weighed down to the point where you don't do many rituals because it's all too much bother is a shame. Recently I wished very much to complete an important ritual, but I knew I would only have half an hour at the most. Using appropriate household ornaments to represent the four elements, and by the light of the Full Moon and an oil-burner, I did what tuned out to be a very effective ritual. Remember, your ritual tools are there to work for you, not to enslave you.

Magical tools may be found. For instance you may find a piece of stone to serve as an athame, or even some wood. In some traditions metal is not allowed in circle, so these would be doubly welcome. The practice of keeping metal out of the circle may relate to its powers to conduct energy or may hark back to Neolithic times, when metal was not used. It is good to be given magical tools as presents, especially by an experienced practitioner.

Study   Try to memorize the essential meanings of the tools and major symbols, refining them with key-words if necessary to help your memory. For instance, the associations for the athame could be shorthanded as Air, concentrate, target (ACT). Use any method that triggers associations for you.

Your tools   Decide what tools you would like to have, and set about acquiring them. To do this you can simply send out a 'call' clearly stating your intention and wish to get a certain implement that will be suitable for your use. By this I mean that you concentrate your mind upon it, inwardly, and then protect this outwards, asking for the help of the Goddess in your undertaking. Probably you will do this instinctively, but if you feel puzzled, don't worry. Usually things will come to you in this way, but if they do not then there is probably a reason. By 'come to you' I do not mean that they materialize by your breakfast plate, but that you come upon them in the course of life, such as finding a wand when out walking. You can also go out and specifically look for articles, in shops, attics and hedgerows. Don't be so intent that you miss other opportunities, however. While you are searching for a cauldron you may come across a beautiful bell instead.

When you find an item, cleanse it in a solution of salt water, and consecrate it to your purpose. We have thus far covered the basics of setting up your circle and invoking the elements, so why not make the consecration of your magical tools your first ritual? Consecrate the implement by offering it to each of the elements/directions in turn, concentrating particularly on the element most relevant. Place your tool on stone or a pentacle for Earth, pass it through incense for Air, through a candle flame for Fire, and immerse it in your chalice for Water. (A good consecration incense mix is sandalwood, frankincense, benzoin and nutmeg.) Visualize the substance in its subtle form entering the tool and purifying it. Place the article in the centre of your circle and dance around it, if you wish, directing the power so raised into the article (see Chapter 8 for further details). Finally, trace the Earth pentagram over the object, with your finger or athame, and put it away with the rest of your special things. Of course, when you start, none of your things will be consecrated, including your chalice, so you will have to content yourself with the use of elements/directions, and your own finger to form a pentagram.

6

THE EIGHT SABBATS

> *Of time you would make a stream upon whose*
> *bank you would sit and watch its flowing.*
> *Yet the timeless in you is aware of life's*
> *timelessness,*
> *And knows that yesterday is but today's memory*
> *and tomorrow is today's dream...*
> *... if in your thoughts you must measure time into*
> *seasons, let each season encircle all the other*
> *seasons,*
> *And let today embrace the past with remembrance*
> *and the future with longing.*

KAHLIL GIBRAN, *THE PROPHET* (1923)

Note: To follow the suggestions for seasonal rituals, you will need to refer to Chapter 8 in respect of raising power, and Chapter 9 for Samhain scrying.

SABBAT AND SEASON

The cycle of the seasons spells out the witches' celebrational passage. In the ever changing, ever renewing face of Nature we see the Goddess and the God. We observe, celebrate, take within, merge with and grow through the natural cycles, for these are the rhythms of our lives and the pulse of the Divine. The power and the beauty of the seasonal spiral is one that you will discover for yourself, as you consciously observe the sabbats, year after year. Each turn of the wheel is another stage on the spiral, a further deepening of awareness and widening of consciousness.

The seasons have mythological and poetic significance, psychological parallels and celebrational inspiration. Each witch comes to know her or his Craft through the 'magic circle' of Nature.

The word *sabbat* means festival, probably derived from the French *s'ebattre* which means 'to frolic'. As special points on the seasonal round, the sabbats may indeed be times for 'frolic' but also for some very serious ritual. Sabbat is the term used for the seasonal festivals marked by the passage of the Sun, whereas *esbat* means a lunar festival, usually at Full Moon. Most traditions observe eight festivals, but not all do, and there may be more then one mythological back-drop to the Sun's journey. The eight sabbats make up the Wheel of the Year. As we experience them, with awareness, and celebrate them in the ways appropriate to our experience, the meanings of the sabbats extend for us, as we also deepen.

Traditionally, pagan worship has two main levels: the esoteric – that is the hidden, inward and mysterious elements embarked upon by mystery traditions such as witchcraft, and the exoteric, which we may understand as the celebrations of the 'ordinary' people. Plenty of significant traditions are still extant, in Christmas celebrations for instance, and in such regional customs as the Abbot's Bromley Horn Dance in England, and similar. We may now add a third dimension, that of the psychological, which is connected to the esoteric. Because of our highly developed individuality and ego-consciousness, the psychological aspect is important, for we question and grow in a way our forbears did not conceive, and as individuals we each have more power and more choice than was enjoyed in historical times. However, the instruction carved over the Eleusinian temple read, 'Know thyself', (see Chapter 1), and so ancient people were well aware of the importance of self-awareness in spiritual progress. This does not mean that we need resort to psychobabble instead of magic. But you cannot

The Wheel of the Year

banish from your circle the unacknowledged demons of your psyche, and passage into the astral takes us through the mists of our own fears and preconceptions. Sometimes, as we travel the Wheel of the Year, we can use the seasonal stations to draw closer to our own essence, and to understand and develop ourselves.

THE FESTIVALS: STORY AND ORIGINS

The eight festivals that we now celebrate are probably an amalgam of Celtic practices and some other traditions from the continent. The cross-quarter festivals of Imbolc, Beltane, Lughnasadh and Samhain are undoubtedly Celtic, important to herding peoples, and times of psychic 'high tide'. At the Equinoxes and Solstices, the tide turns. These are astronomical dates, when the sun moves into one of the cardinal signs, Capricorn, Aries, Cancer and Libra, and while the precise date does vary a little from year to year, there is no doubt about fixity and exactitude in terms of solar movement. On the other hand, the cross-quarter festivals have no such marker, and while we do define dates, these may not have been marked with rigid reference to a calendar, but more by the seasonal 'feel'. In addition, it is probable that all the festivals were celebrated over a period of several days. Some sources state that the phase of the Moon was operational, thus the festival would have been celebrated at the nearest Full or New Moon. Witches these days tend to celebrate when convenient, usually at the weekend closest to the festival. Occult tradition does suggest that it is better to celebrate later, rather than earlier, as then you are riding with the tide, not pre-empting it. However, you also may go by 'feel' if you wish.

The old pagan festivals were taken over by the Church and incorporated into its calendar, in order to induce the population to follow. Samhain, Feast of the Dead, thus became All Hallow's E'en, the day before All Saints, and then All Souls. Christmas took over from Yule, as the birth of the Sun God was instead the birth of Christ, and Imbolc became Candlemas and so forth.

The following lists all the festivals and their dates:
Yule/Midwinter: 22 December, Imbolc: 2 February, Spring Equinox: 21 March, Beltane: 30 April, Midsummer: 22 June, Lughnasadh/Lammas: 31 July, Autumn Equinox: 21 September, Samhain/Hallowe'en: 31 October. Readers in the southern hemisphere will probably like to move the dates around by half a year, so that Yule is celebrated on or around 22 June, and so forth. As you can see from the illustration, the Wheel of the Year corresponds to the phases of the Moon, points on the compass and others, tying in with other concepts of ritual and magical circles.

There are overlaps, parallels and paradoxes in the seasonal story, but we may understand it something like this:
At Yule, when the Sun turns in the sky, beginning his slow progress back to light and life, the Goddess gives birth to the magical babe, who is the God. We may also understand it as Her rebirthing Herself, so that as the pale Spring light grows, She too grows into the Maiden. At Imbolc we may see the Goddess both as young Mother and also as Maiden. This is a creative time of purgings, beginnings, growing strength. The God, in the secret places of Nature, is young and wild. At Spring Equinox we have a festival that celebrates the fertility of the plant kingdom, while the God and Goddess are youthful and full of potential. Perhaps they mate at this time, but there is no commitment, only enjoyment of life. At Beltane, the Goddess and God come to maturity and celebrate their union with passion and joy. With Beltane we have the festival, par excellence, of human sexuality. At Midsummer, the Goddess is pregnant and glowing in all the splendid blooms and lush greenery of Nature. However, although Midsummer is the peak of light, now darkness begins to grow. By this token the God turns

His face inward, to His responsibilities as co-guardian of Nature, to His journey and His coming demise. At the end of August, at Lughnasadh, He is cut down with the corn, as the Corn Spirit, and begins His underworld descent, although He is also, in a sense, immediately born again, in the harvest produce. Autumn Equinox is another harvest celebration. Now the Goddess is left alone, or we may see the God arising from the Underworld to claim Her, as Pluto did with Persephone. The turn of the season is both bountiful, and sad, and a reflective time steals over us. At Samhain the God stands enthroned as Underworld King and the Goddess reigns beside Him in the dark realms before His departure out of the world of Time. Or we may see the Goddess now as Wise Crone, who presides over the deepening year. At Yule, the God is reborn in the person of His own son, and so the spiral unfolds.

Not all traditions depict the cycle in the same way. To some the Lady sleeps in Winter, while the God stands guardian of the Wildwood, the hibernating creatures and the seeds snuggling deep within the earth. At the appropriate time the Lady wakes, and the Lord spreads His green mantle in welcome. Not all traditions have eight sabbats. This is described by Rhiannon Ryall in *West Country Wicca* (see Further Reading). In addition, the seasonal story, as I have given it, is very heterosexual, and while witches may see that creative male-female polarity is the basis for the manifest world, this polarity is present in homosexual relationships, also. You may evolve a story, or draw on whatever mythology you wish to evoke the feeling of the seasons for you. However, I believe the eight sabbats are a good and traditional framework, not to be put aside lightly.

HOLLY KING AND OAK KING

While the Goddess is always with us, changing Her face, but not Her essence, the God presents more contrasts. It is necessary for the initiating, conquest-oriented spirit of the Masculine to be prepared to die, to go within, to give up, depart, and only in due time regenerate. Our culture, patriarchal and lop-sided as it is, does not include this, emphasizing instead the importance of continual economic growth, sky-scrapers that go higher and higher, and men who expect themselves to be always assertive and sexually ready (to the current delight of the drug companies!). The example of the God may be a message to men that it is okay to go within, to be weak sometimes, gentle and introverted, to let go in order, eventually, to move on. It also portrays the paradox of Nature, where there are beginnings and endings, some of them bitter, but in the end all is the same.

As a cycle within a cycle, we have also the persons of the Holly King and the Oak King, aspects of the God that battle for the favour of the Lady. At Yule, Oak King wins, and he reigns as Lord of the Waxing Year, until Midsummer, when again they fight and Holly wins, to preside as Lord of the Waning Year. This myth reappears in various forms, for instance in the Arthurian story of Gawain and the Green Knight. Always, behind the scenes, the Goddess is guiding, for She knows what must be. She is initiatrix and prize. The 'dark' side of the God is not, of course, evil, but has meanings of inwardness and perhaps necessary destruction, in order that the process of Life may continue to unfold. Wiccan rituals at Yule and Midsummer usually include an enactment of the fight between Oak and Holly, and you may wish to incorporate this idea into your individual rituals.

SAMHAIN

Looking at the festivals in their proper order, let us start with Samhain, which is the Celtic New Year. Please note, accounts of Wiccan rituals are not complete, but are included to give an idea and a 'flavour'. Samhain is usually pronounced 'sa-wain', meaning 'summer's end'. For the Celts it was the beginning of the year. Darkness was a time of beginnings, and day began at nightfall. This Celtic attitude is important and relevant for witches, for to these people Otherworld was a reality, and the Land of the Dead was also called the Land of the Living. The Celtic sense of 'reality' was a mystical one, embracing an understanding of the value of death and the importance of cycle. This can be seen in aspects of Celtic culture: Celtic knotwork is continuous, and Celtic music comes to no natural end, but just stops (because, for practical purposes, one has to stop somewhere). In this way the eternal cycle is reflected.

Samhain is the year's truly 'darkest' time, because at Yule, when nights are longest, the reign of darkness is ending, and its peak is its vanquishing. But at Samhain the trough of the year lies before us. In times of yore this was indeed a fearful time, when the old and the sickly might not see another Spring, when difficult and harsh decisions had to be reached about which livestock were to be kept through the Winter and which killed and salted, how much harvest produce might be needed to withstand the Winter and what might be bartered. Wrong decisions might mean death to the individual and even whole family.

The scary shiver we experience, deliciously, as the wind moans into the darkening evenings, is a relic of the dread felt by the ancients, and one response to this was the offering of sacrifices, including human ones, as propitiation. Often it was the king who was ritually sacrificed, to return to the Goddess, who was the land, and by whose authority, and no other, he held office. This is interestingly echoed by our ritual burning of Guy Fawkes, on 5 November. Instead of the king, a would-be king-slayer goes on the bonfire. When Guy Fawkes tried to blow up parliament on 4 November 1605, was he unconsciously influenced by older traditions? James I was an example of the paranoid type of king who ruled by divine right, the tyrant Holdfast, who would not let go or submit to natural cycle, but who arrogantly proclaimed his royalty. It was his son, Charles I, who paid with his life and his head.

Samhain was also a time of misrule, similar to the Roman festival of Saturnialia, when chaos reigned pending a new beginning. This survives today as 'trick or treat', an American custom which has reappeared in Britain, but which derives from older European practices. Trick or treat honours the trickiness of the season and the human being, as we are not creatures of light and life alone, but we all have our darker side. Not that we have *carte blanche* for rampant indulgence of any murderous impulses, but we may allow these elements into our consciousness for balance. Samhain is a time of hauntings, when the spirits of the dead may seek the warmth of the hearth, and passage into and out of the world of Faerie is smoothly accomplished, with no password. It was the start of the Celtic season of story-telling, when old heroes were remembered and new ones conjured into life. The tradition of the pumpkin lantern is the face of the Crone, to frighten away demons, but we welcome the return of the Beloved Dead, especially into our ritual circle, if they wish to honour us.

Samhain falls in the middle of the sign Scorpio, and the Samhain themes of death and transformation are appropriate to this sign. Also known for its sexuality, Scorpio brings us the message of how our sexuality can take us into our own 'underworld' and bring us to transformative stages. It is well known that being a little bit scared can make us feel sexy, and Samhain honours this shadowy aspect, as the mirror-image of the delicious sensuality of Beltane, its opposite on the Wheel.

Things to do

Tell stories, especially ghostly ones, with family or friends, remember the dead, visit barrow mounds, standing stones and graveyards (perhaps in mist, or rain, or sheltering from the wind behind a hood). Scrying is traditional at this time (see Chapter 9 for a full description) and is best done in circle. Reflect on what needs to be let go of in life and face inner demons and fears. More frivolous but still meaningful, apple-bobbing at a Hallowe'en party is symbolic of the descent into the Underworld, as portrayed by the water, which is also the water of the unconscious and the emotional and imaginal world. Apples are a magical fruit of the Underworld and the realms of Faerie. Cut an apple in half crossways and you will see at the centre the five-point star of the Goddess. Always hollow out a pumpkin. These are easier to cut into than the traditional British turnip and nothing evokes the season more immediately.

Samhain ritual

The following is a brief summery of a Samhain ritual in a Wiccan coven. A slow dance may be undertaken, around the circle, chanting the Witches' Rune (see Chapter 8). The High Priest takes on the persona of the God, standing in the West of the circle, which is the direction of the Islands of the Blessed, where the dead have departed. The High Priestess summons the great Horned God from His Underworld abode with the words:

> *Agency of ineffable name and vast strength*
> *Ancient dark one, thou cold barren and mournful*
> *Whose word is as stone and whose life is abiding*
> *And whose holy night we now celebrate, where are you!*
> *Giver of peace and rest be present, we pray you.*

Facing the High Priest as embodiment of the God, the High Priestess honours him, saying:

> *Dread Lord of Shadows, God of Life and the Giver of*
> *Life, yet is the knowledge of thee the knowledge of*
> *Death, open wide, I pray thee, the gates through*
> *which all must pass. Let our dear ones who have gone*

before us return this night to make merry with us. And when our time comes, as it must, O thou Comforter, Consoler, Giver of Peace and Rest, we will enter thy realms gladly and unafraid.

For we know that when rested and refreshed among dear ones, we will be reborn again of thy grace, and the grace of the Great Mother. Let it be in the same place and the same time as our beloved ones, and may we meet and know and remember, and love them again.

Descend, we pray thee, on thy servant and priest.

After honouring the God the coven may sit around the cauldron in the centre of the circle. Incense may have been lit in the cauldron, and now all can gaze into the smoke, or scry with a stone or crystal. The Great Rite, which is a symbolic depiction of the act of sexual union, using an athame and a chalice of wine, is enacted by the High Priest and Priestess, the former lowering his athame into the chalice, held by his partner. The chalice is than passed man to woman, woman to man, around the coven, with a kiss each time. Cakes are also consecrated and shared. The proceedings are concluded with games and jokes, in an unruly mood to suit the season.

If you are celebrating alone, or with a group, you may wish to use some of the above as inspiration. You will always need to observe the routine for creating your circle, summoning the Guardians at each of the four quarters etc., before embarking on your ritual. Invoke also the Goddess and the God, by saying something like:

Great and glorious Mother
Whose mantle is the stars, whose body is the green earth
By the mystery of the waters
By the pulse of my blood
By the beauty of life and love
I ask your presence.

Feel the glow and bounty of the Great Mother flow around you and into your circle. Invite now the God:

> *Mighty Horned One*
> *God of Nature, the rising sap, the rutting stag*
> *By corn and seed*
> *By horn, bone, soil and stone*
> *And by lust and laughter*
> *I ask for your presence.*

Feel the energy and vitality of the God enter you and your circle like lightning. Substitute words of your own choosing if you do not like the above. Proceed when you are ready to the rest of your prepared ritual. When you have completed your ritual work, always finish off thoroughly and ground yourself. Here are some themes you may wish to include.

Candles should be predominantly black. The altar should display such items as nuts, especially on the twig, apples cut crossways, a hollowed-out pumpkin, evergreen fronds, holly, pine cones. The cauldron should ideally figure promininetly, as a receptacle for transformation/rebirth and a source of inspiration. The Welsh Goddess Cerridwen is often thought of at Samhain, as a representation of the Dark Goddess. She brewed a magical broth to endow her son with wisdom, but droplets spilt on the finger of Gwion Bach, whom she had set to stir it. She pursued Gwion in a shape-shifting chase, and when he finally turned into a grain of wheat, she turned into a hen and ate him, later giving birth to the bard Taliesin.

In your ritual you may like to honour the God in His Underworld aspect, by lighting a black candle in the West, saying words of your choosing. Scrying and communing with the Beloved Dead and the spirits of your ancestors could form part of your ritual. Take time to meditate on the meaning of this time. Psychologically it may be a time of letting go, in some sense, and you may like to mark this ritually by unravelling a spiral of thread and burning it.

Consecrate wine and cakes to the Goddess and God in the Underworld, and don't forget to leave outside an offering to the Sidhe, the people of Faerie, who are close tonight. At some point it is good to put out all the candles save one, placed perhaps in the cauldron. Savour the depth of darkness before relighting other candles from the one in the cauldron. As you may feel quiet at this festival, you may choose to raise power by chanting and swaying, in a sitting position, perhaps directing the power into knotting and weaving three strands of black thread. These could represent three things that need to go from life. Your theme could be cruelty, and you might incorporate a humanitarian issue, something for a friend and something for yourself (most of us are cruel to ourselves, even if no one else is!). Place a final knot in your threads and burn them in your cauldron. Celebrate the continuing life, as it recedes to hide beneath the earth, and celebrate the inner fires of the spirit. This may be done by anointing a candle with oils of myrrh and sandalwood, and ritually igniting it. Or, for the same symbolism, you could choose to light the candle in your pumpkin as part of the ritual. As Samhain rites are sombre, always reaffirm life at the close, consecrating red wine and rich fruit cake, and eating and drinking in celebration of the Goddess and the God, in the gentle realms of night. Samhain is especially sexy, so make love, in your circle if you are working with a partner, or share your remaining wine in bed with your lover, after you have properly closed down your circle.

YULE

Now is the time of rebirth of the Sun God, born again of the Great Mother, as the light slowly returns on the barren landscape of Winter. In many mythologies the theme of the dying and resurrecting God is prominently featured, and it is no accident that the feast of Christmas was positioned at the Winter Solstice, to coincide with earlier observances. While in many cultures the Sun was feminine, today even very feminist witches tend to regard the Sun as generally masculine in essence, dying and resurrecting as it does, while the land as Goddess is ever with us. Much of the Christmas symbolism is pagan in essence, for the evergreen Christmas tree is a Goddess object, and the fairy on the treetop is the Goddess Herself! Gifts given to friends and family are the gifts for the Divine Child, and all the lights and the brightness are an instinctual response, to conjure the return of the life-giving Sun. Red and gold, favourites for decorations, are solar colours. Even Father Christmas, with his reindeer, has links with the Horned God, who was later subverted as 'the devil' and called Old Nick. Santa Claus and Saint Nick are other names for Father Christmas, who may also have links with the German Goddess Holda, who came down the chimney dressed in red and bearing gifts. Father Christmas may also be an Oak King figure.

All the principle festivals were Fire festivals, although at Yule this appears as the Yule log, because conditions would have been too inclement to kindle fire. There are many traditions attached to this. Some say the Yule log should be ash; others oak. A piece of the Yule log should be kept, to kindle the Yule log the following year. Often today our only remnant of the Yule log is a table decoration, or a chocolate log, but in olden times this log meant the rekindling of light and life.

The Holy Family in their stable are an ancient and meaningful group and the animals that are involved in the story: the ox and the ass, and the shepherds with their sheep are all an epiphany of the Goddess. The ox may be linked to the Bull, sacred to the Goddess in Cretan culture. Witches need not feel that a Christmas crib is irrelevant, for Mary in her blue robe is the Goddess indeed, Joseph is the shadowy presence of the old God, and the babe is the Sun god, complete with a halo of solar rays.

Things to do

All the usual Christmas traditions can be celebrated with new vigour as their pagan and witchy significance is appreciated. Holly and mistletoe can be hung as a salute to Holly King and Oak King, for mistletoe was most prized by the Druids when it grew on the oak. Mistletoe, because it grows and is a fully fledged plant, but does not touch the ground, symbolizes the entry into Time, the moment of incarnation. Druids reverently cut the mistletoe with a golden sickle, thereby honouring Sun and Moon, Feminine and Masculine, and distribute it as a symbol of fertility and wisdom – so to kiss under the mistletoe is a meaningful spell. Holly is special for men, and ivy is for women, carried by each for good luck, and to deck our homes with these is a good old fertility theme. You might like to join in a wassail, if you live in an apple-growing region. This is a ceremony to wake up the trees with singing and dancing, offering cider as a libation to the roots (and drinking lots of it, too!). If possible you may like to visit certain barrow mounds that are constructed so that the rays of the Sun penetrate to the heart of the earth, at the Winter Solstice. One notable example is New Grange, in Northern Ireland. Another is found at Stony Littleton in Somerset, England. You might like to do a little research in your local area, where there are standing stones and mounds, or simply go along to absorb the essence of the earth as it resonates to the turn of the tide and the approach of the Sun.

Yule ritual

Wiccan rituals will place the cauldron towards the South of the circle, wreathed in seasonal greenery, with a fire within. All other light is kept to a minimum. The High Priestess stands behind the cauldron and the High Priest faces her, with a bundle of unlit candles. The coven circle slowly, deosil, around the cauldron and the High Priest hands each

one in turn a lighted candle, kindled from the cauldron.
While the coven continue to circle he reads the following:

> *Queen of the Moon, Queen of the Sun*
> *Queen of the Heavens, Queen of the Stars*
> *Queen of the Waters, Queen of the Earth*
> *Bring to us the Child of Promise*
> *It is the Great Mother who giveth birth to him*
> *It is the Lord of Life who is born again*
> *Darkness and tears are set aside*
> *When the Sun shall come up early*
> *Golden Sun of the mountains*
> *Illumine the land, light up the world*
> *Illumine the seas and the rivers*
> *Sorrows be laid, joy to the world*
> *Blessed Be the Great Goddess, without*
>   *beginning, without end*
> *Everlasting to eternity*
> *Lo! Evo! He! Blessed Be.*

The chant is taken up by the coven and power is raised until
the High Priestess calls an end. Other matters follow,
including an enactment of the struggle of Holly and Oak
King, with cakes and wine consecrated. The cauldron is
moved to the centre and everyone jumps over it. Ashes of
the Yule log may be scattered over the garden or fields on
the following day.

For your celebration, alone or in a group, choose candles of
red and green. Deck your altar with holly, ivy and mistletoe.
You might also have a Christmas crib there, placing an
effigy of the Babe in his crib as a focal point of the ritual.
Naturally you may choose suitably pagan figures for the
Goddess, perhaps a statue of Isis, with any representation of
the adult God very much in the background, for now He is
reborn as baby. Have a special large Sun candle within your
cauldron, to light as a focus of your ritual. From this you
may light other candles, perhaps eight, for each station of

the Wheel of the Year in its eight sabbats, or four for each of
the quarters, or whatever seems appropriate. Dance around
your circle, ringing a bell and calling, 'Wake up land, sea
and sky! The brightness of the reborn Sun calls out to the
return of life, new growth, a new year. Blessed be the Great
Mother, Blessed be the Sun God, child of promise.' You may
wish to substitute your own words. You may enact the
battle of Oak and Holly by using candles of red and green.
Light the red candle of Oak from a dark green candle, for
Holly, and put out the flame of Holly's candle, saying,
'Farewell my Lord of Holly, guard the dark realms until our
return. Well met, my Lord of Oak. Guard close the Lady,
and the Magical Babe, as the year unfolds.'

Move your cauldron with its large Sun candle within to the
centre of your circle and watch the flame. Think about what
is being reborn in you. Pledge a gift to the Goddess and
God. Consecrate wine and food to the Goddess and drink in
celebration of the Sun's return. You may wish to make a
golden crown before your ritual and place it upon your
head, as you face South, looking into the flame of your Sun
candle. (If you are working with other people, you may take
it in turns to be 'crowned'.) As you feel the crown upon your
head, feel the warmth, joy and triumph of the returning Sun
in your life, and count all the gifts that you have. Pictures of
a special gift from the Goddess for you may arise, or during
pathworking (see Chapter 9) this may be revealed. Save
wine or juice to pour later upon the soil, celebrate and
commune, inwardly drawing close to the Goddess and the
new Babe. Close down in the usual fashion.

IMBOLC

The literal meaning of *Imbolc* is 'in the belly'. It is deep
within the belly of earth that life now stirs, in response to
lengthening days. The first lambs are born and the ewe's

milk flows in reply. The first Spring flowers brave the bitter winds, and we catch glimpses of the Goddess as Bright Maiden. However, She does not radiate quite the gentleness and serenity of balmier days. At this time of growing light, She is energetic and demanding, vibrant with creativity. In earlier times this was a favourite festival for initiation of priestesses. It is especially linked with the celtic goddess, Bride (pronounced 'Breed') who later evolved into the Irish St Bridget. Bride presides over all kinds of creativity, smithcraft, poetry, childbirth, goddess of the hearth and Keeper of the Sacred Flame. Imbolc was also called The Feast of the Poets. Interestingly, the Scottish Burn's night falls a week before Imbolc.

Bride is known as a Triple Goddess, embodying Maiden, Mother and Crone in Her person and thus including inspiration, fertility and inner knowledge among her gifts. One of the customs special to Imbolc was that of the Bridie Doll, or Bride Doll, which can be anything from last year's Corn Dolly wrapped in a scarf to a richly dressed, beautiful doll. In some places the Bride Doll was 'put to bed' with a phallic piece of wood, and left there all night with candles burning beside her. If an impression of a club, or phallus, was to be found in the ashes in the hearth next morning, this was an indication of good fortunes. Some customs return the Bridie to the earth, but these are evolving in ways suitable to our times. In the House of the Goddess (see Resources) each woman takes it in turns to go to bed with the Bridie doll and tell of her childbirth or motherhood experiences and feelings. In Glastonbury, England, the Bridie of the year is introduced to other Bridies of earlier years, at a ceremony at the sacred well, thus passing wisdom and tradition on.

Imbolc was incorporated into the Christian festival of Candlemas, the feast of the Purification of the Virgin Mary. (Modern mothers may see the link here with the 'six-week check up'!) While candles are vital at all the festivals, they are especially important at Imbolc.

Things to do

You may like to visit wells, rivers or lakes, as symbols of the healing powers of the Goddess. Because this is a festival of creativity, you may like to explore art galleries and craft centres. Light a festive white candle and think about the things you would like to do, to develop and create in the coming year. Plan projects with friends, if you like, perhaps a collective task such as reclaiming land that has become overgrown, holding an evening of poetry or literature, perhaps on a Goddess theme, or making a patchwork quilt together and raffling it for charity. Identify a creative talent that you have and decide that you will work at it over the coming year.

Imbolc ritual

Dancing is a special feature of this festival in Wiccan groups, and the High Priestess may head this, carrying the wand, and using a chant of her own choice. The High Priest stands before the altar, and the High Priestess, facing him, says:

> *Dread Lord of Death and Resurrection, of Life, and the Giver of Life, Lord within ourselves whose name is the Mystery of Mysteries, encourage our hearts.*

> *Let the light crystallize itself in our blood, fulfilling of us resurrection, for there is no part of us that is not of the Gods. Descend we pray thee upon thy servant and priest.*

The High Priest draws the Earth-invoking pentagram in the air, before the High Priestess, saying, 'Blessed Be'.

The Bride Doll can now be put into 'bed' by the women of the coven. The High Priestess and two other women now enact The Triple Goddess, the Mother being crowned with a crown of light. (Birthday candles can be used here, but obviously considerable care and skill needs to be used in the making of a headdress using real flame or bulbs!) Facing the triple grouping the High Priest says:

> *Behold the Three-Formed Goddess*
> *She who is ever three, Maid, Mother and Crone*
> *Yet is She ever One*
> *For without Spring there can be no Summer*
> *Without Summer, no Winter, without Winter,*
>   *no new Spring.*

The circle is ritually swept by the Maid. Cakes and wine follow.

Whether you are performing a solo or group ritual, be sure to feature white candles, in the spirit of this bright festival. A white altar cloth covering some of the space can set the scene, with some evergreen fronds. All should be bright, clear and clean. Some early-flowering fragrant hyacinths would be very appropriate, especially white ones, growing in a bowl. Imbolc is an excellent time to renew your commitment to the Goddess by anointing yourself, in circle, with lavender oil on forehead, lips and breast, just above your genitals, knees and feet. You may light three candles in honour of the Triple Goddess, or place nine small ones around your Goddess figure and light them, one by one, deosil, saying something like:

> *Blessed Be the Maid, the Mother and the Crone.*
> *Blessed Be the Three-Formed Goddess. I welcome the*
> *growth of light, I honour the Triple Goddess and I ask*
> *that creativity may grow within me.*

You may like to sweep out your circle, widdershins (opposite to deosil). Name the things which you are sweeping away, such as guilt, fear, or cruelty. Again, a good tradition is to name one thing for yourself, another for a friend, and another for the world. Throw down dried leaves in front of your broom, to represent what you are 'sweeping' and burn them later. Dance around your cauldron, in which you have placed a large white candle, chanting:

Light come, light grow
Sun shine, candle glow
Flowers bloom, milk flow
Light come, light grow.

Direct power into the candle and light it in honour of all positive acts, everywhere (or something more specific, if you wish) and in honour of the Goddess. From this candle you may light others around your circle, or if possible, perform this part of the ritual first, after your Goddess and God invocations, and then you can light your three candles to the Triple Goddess from the cauldron candle. Lay upon your altar, before your Goddess figure, something creative you have done in the last year, from knitting, sewing, poetry, pottery through to exam certificates gained. Commune, reflect and close. If you are lucky enough to have an open fire, use your cauldron candle to kindle this. Take your candle, or several candles with the Goddess figure, on a tray, with salt and water, and purify and consecrate all the rooms in your house, in honour of the Triple Goddess and the growth of Spring.

SPRING EQUINOX

At Spring Equinox day and night are of equal length all over the world, but light is gaining. Now is primarily the feast of the fertility of vegetation. Themes mingle, for Spring comes at different times across the globe and the Sacred Marriage of Goddess and God, which underlines all seasons of course, is paramount. As befits the atmosphere of being on the brink, at the turn of the tide that characterizes the Equinoxes, this is a paradoxical time as well as a time to celebrate the growth of life and the approach of Summer. Older pagan rites, such as the cult of the goddess Cybele and her lover Attis, were celebrated at this time, with priests castrating themselves in a brutal ceremony. The theme of sacrifice as well as celebration abounds at this ambiguous time. Sacrifice, which primarily arises from fear and alienation from our Source, is not required by modern pagans. However, it is worth remembering at this time of rebirth, that new growth has been fertilized, by the mulch of last year's dead leaves.

Life now resurrects from the crypt of Winter, and by the same token, the Christian tradition celebrates the resurrection of Christ at Easter, which takes place on the first Sunday after the first Full Moon after the Spring Equinox. Easter is named after the Goddess Eostre, a Teutonic goddess of fertility, in whose honour eggs were hidden and hunted. This custom survives in some cultures, where eggs are hidden by the Easter Bunny so that children can look for them on Easter morning. Fertility symbols abound here, in defiance of biology! Eostre's name gives us our word for 'oestrogen', the egg-stimulating hormone.

At this point in the year the Sun, as the young God growing to manhood, receives His arms. Golden daffodils wave, five-petaled primroses honour the Goddess. Newness, brightness and promise are in the air. The symbol that is favourite at this time is the wheel, with four or eight spokes, to mark the round of the Sun, the four quarters/eight festivals and the triumphal passage of the Sun.

Things to do

You may like to bring Spring flowers into your home in pots, and plant them outside as the weather grows warm. Decorate eggs for family and friends using food colouring. Clean the house in the tradition of Spring cleaning or go out into the country and enjoy the springing into life of Nature. Plant a tree, or plant seeds. Make hot cross buns as symbols of the quartered circle and an edible Solar Wheel.

Spring Equinox ritual

Celebrating the Wiccan way will probably involve placing a golden disc, or wheel, on the altar and flanking it with candles. The High Priest stands on the East while the High Priestess faces him. They both hold wands, and the High Priestess says:

> We kindle this fire today in the presence of the
>   Holy Ones
> Without malice, without jealousy, without envy
> Without fear of aught beneath the sun by the
>   High Gods
> Thee we invoke O light of Life
> Be thou a bright flame before us
> Be thou a guiding star above us
> Be thou a smooth path beneath us
> Kindle thou within our hearts a flame
> Of love for our neighbours, to our foes
> To our friends, to our kindred all
> To all men on the broad earth
> O merciful son of Cerridwen
> From the lowliest thing that liveth
> To the name which is highest of all.

In the air, before the High Priest, the High Priestess traces the Earth-invoking pentagram and hands him her wand as a sign of the growing solar power. A lighted taper is presented to the High Priest, who then lights a fire/candle in the cauldron. The coven dance, taking it in turns to jump the cauldron, making a wish.

When composing your own ritual, choose candles of bright yellow or Spring green and deck your altar with spring flowers in pots. Include eggs, hard-boiled and painted, on your altar, and after consecrating these you can give them to friends and family. It is lovely also to fill your cauldron with blooms, such as daffodils, with a central candle. Dance around your circle, imagining the power rising in a cone, and when ready direct this towards a suitable cause. When you light the candle in your cauldron, take time to visualize the growth of new life, bringing peace and brightness to the world. Crouch by your cauldron facing East, slowly uncurl and stand, raising your arms and holding them wide and aloft, welcoming new life into your heart and soul. Move through each of the four quarters, visualizing the gifts of the elemental spirits entering you and 'hatching' within you, and also breaking out in golden showers over the world. You may feel new realizations dawning within you, and if so take note of these in your Book of Shadows before closing your circle, otherwise you may forget them. Consecrate a raw egg to a growth in human consciousness. After your ritual, take the egg into garden or parkland (or window box) and break it into the soil, stirring it with a stick and crumpling the shell, also into the earth. Say, 'May new awareness hatch, in love and light, for humankind, and for the planet, in the name of the Great Mother and the Horned God. Blessed Be.'

BELTANE

Beltane is the most joyful of the festivals, gleefully sensual, celebrating the fertility of human, animal and the plant kingdom, and the union of Goddess and God. The days seem full of promise and the nights full of magic. Nature is vibrant and beautiful. The Sacred Marriage of the Goddess as the land and the God as the life force is now celebrated. At this festival, witchcraft makes a clear statement about the sacredness of sexuality and physical joy, as gifts of the Goddess. While we do not precisely wish for an increase in population these days, fertility is not merely a matter of procreation, but also involves spirit, mind and soul. With this in mind, witchcraft's 'fertility cult' aspect is highlighted, and revelled in. Both Goddess and God are filled with the vigour and potential of young adulthood. In days of old, young people would stay out all night, going a-maying, which meant gathering hawthorn, unlucky if brought in before May Eve, and no doubt making love in the Spring dusk. So-called 'woodland weddings' took place on May Eve, when the couple would jump a fire for good luck. As the Celtic start of Summer, Beltane was possibly the most important of the festivals, and definitely a fire festival. Cattle were driven through the ashes of the Beltane fire, for purification. Bel, who gave his name to the festival, was a god of brightness, and fire, and in his honour beacons were lit on the hilltops to signal that the Sun had come to earth.

One of the most well-known Beltane customs is that of the maypole, around which people dance, weaving the ribbons that extend from the top in a way suggesting the spiral of life. The phallic symbolism of this is obvious, and was probably one of the reasons why the maypole was banned by the Puritans until Charles II brought it back, along with the spirit of fun and enjoyment. Another custom was to crown a pretty girl as Queen of the May, in celebration of the Maiden aspect of the Goddess. This is connected with Maid Marion, of English folklore, who is really the Maiden goddess of the wild and secret places of Nature, while her consort, Robin Hood, is the great god Pan himself, in disguise! Beltane was a time of riot and mischief, similar to Samhain, when anything might happen, and when the doors of Otherworld were ajar. Merry customs, such as that of the Padstow 'Obby 'Oss in England, still survive in honour of this time. Mythologically, this time marked the coming of the Gaels to the shores of Ireland, denoting in fact the union of humankind with the land itself as Goddess. As they landed, their bard, Amergin, proclaimed one of the most evocative of pagan litanies:

> *I am a stag; of seven tines*
> *I am a flood; across a plain*
> *I am a wind; on a deep lake*
> *I am a tear; the sun lets fall …*

> *I am a wonder; among flowers*
> *I am a wizard; who but I*
> *Sets the cool head aflame with smoke.*

This is produced in its entirety in *The White Goddess* (see Further Reading) and it can form an inspiring background when creating your own rituals. Beltane is the festival to glory in all the gifts of the Goddess, including our own bodies, and to celebrate the sacred aspect of sexuality.

Things to do

Now is the time to get out and about anywhere. Have a party, or a barbecue if the weather is warm. Treat yourself to something that is physically indulgent like a massage, facial or aromatherapy. Go dancing, or do something adventurous. Have a really wonderful meal, and generally enjoy things of beauty and delight. Make love.

Beltane ritual

Decorate your altar with hawthorn and late Spring flowers, or any seasonal greenery. You may also like to place oak leaves, if you can get some. Wiccan rituals for this time are infused with as much fun as possible. The High Priestess and High Priest enact a 'love-chase', where he pursues her, trying to catch her with a scarf, while she eludes him. After she allows him to capture her, other coven members may follow suit, playing out the mock chase in pairs. Then the High Priest pursues the High Priestess once more, but this time in more solemn fashion, and when he 'catches' her, he 'dies' as the God dies in the arms of the Goddess, to be reborn in greater consciousness. The candle, previously lit in the cauldron, is blown out and rekindled in order that the Oak King may be revived. The High Priest, as the God/Oak King, comes back to life when he accepts a candle ignited from the cauldron. The candle in the cauldron is an indoor substitute for the Bel-fire, the fire of life. The High Priest may now proclaim some of the Song of Amergin.

The coven now dance around the cauldron. In come covens poles are ridden, as hobbyhorses are a feature of several contemporary May Eve customs – the meaning here being obvious! The chant is borrowed from Kipling:

> *Oh do not tell the priest of our art for he would*
> *call it sin*
> *But we will be in the woods all night a-*
> *conjuring Summer in*
> *And we bring you good news*
> *For women and cattle and corn*
> *For the sun is coming up from the South*
> *With Oak and Ash and Thorn.*

The cauldron flame is jumped for good luck, as a substitute for the Bel-fire, and feasting follows.

My choice for Beltane candles are deep rose-pink or crimson, with a fat, orange Sun candle in the cauldron, surrounded by rose petals. You may dance, raising power for a suitable cause and directing it into the rose petals, which you could later scatter outside. Themes such as respect for Nature in all her forms, love, warmth and acceptance are suggested, especially a balanced, healthy attitude to sex. A bowl of soft compost could be consecrated, in circle, and decorated with fresh flowers. You may place a short stick or prepared wand (gathered from fallen wood) in the compost saying something like:

> *As the staff is to the Earth, so the male is to the*
> *female. In peace and love may they unite, bringing joy*
> *to the world, as the Sun lights up the hills and valleys*
> *and the blossoms flourish. Blessed Be.*

You could then decorate your planted staff with coloured thread or ribbon, each for a specific wish. Raise more power for this, by dancing and/or chanting, if you wish. Make sure your ribbons or threads are bio-degradable and bury compost, staff and ribbons outside after your ritual. Even better, deck the staff with flowers. Sit quietly and meditate on the life force that is growing, the power and meaning of your own sexuality, and visualize the power or sunlight flowing forth and blessing the welcoming land. Have some specially chosen wine and edible goodies to consecrate, and eat and drink in honour of the union of Goddess and God. In time, close down as usual.

MIDSUMMER

This is the peak of the year, where day seems to extend into day, separated only by a balmy dusk, and riotous blooms proclaim the fertility of the earth. Midsummer is possibly the most ambiguous festival, for while everywhere there is bountiful testimony of the powers of light and life, yet at this point light begins to wane and the slow journey into darkness begins. At the height of his power, the Oak King is slain by his alter ego, Holly King. Goddess and God, fulfilled by their union, begin to change. The Goddess evolves from Maiden to Mother, and the God, conscious of His responsibility and of the mortality inherent within all life, turns ever inward. Inspired by His love he embarks on a quest, which is the true hero's quest, facing the darkness within, and as in the external world, light begins slowly to wane and the inner light grows.

One myth illustrates the theme of the hero's descent beautifully, and it is the story of Theseus, who defeats the horrific half-man, half-bull Minotaur, deep within the labyrinth of the Cretan tyrant, Minos. Theseus succeeds with the help of Ariadne, daughter to Minos, who is part of a tradition of weaving goddesses, such as Arachne, Athene, and Arianrhod. Ariadne gives him a thread to unwind, and so he is able to find his way back, his prize being Ariadne herself. There are many themes here. Just as the Goddess is herself the cycle, through which the Sun God travels, so the Goddess in this story is the labyrinth, the advisor and the prize. Even the Minotaur partakes of Her, and of the God, for the head of a bull forms a similar cross-section to the womb and ovaries, long horns mimicking the sweeping Fallopian tubes, and in historical Crete the bull was seen as the Sun/Lover of the Goddess. The point is not so much that Theseus kills the Minotaur, but that he goes down to meet it and takes on its power, which is the power of his own instinctual Self, now conjoined to his conscious Self. So his experience is of initiation, at the hands of the Goddess. While there is no mention of the Holy Grail or similar, in this story, the Grail cup (being far older than Christianity) signifies the gifts of the Goddess.

I am not aware of any traditions for initiations of male priests at Midsummer, although there were probably ritual sacrifices of the king, or a substitute, enacting Oak King. The Feast of St John the Baptist, losing his head on 24 June, echoes this. Midsummer is both a Fire and a Water festival, twin fires representing the dual aspect of the God, and water representing the Goddess. The arms of the Goddess are now full of gifts, but She also issues a challenge, and at Her brightest time She is also death-in-life.

Things to do

Go on a pilgrimage to some special ancient site, such as a stone circle. Such circles are often built to herald the rise of the Sun on Midsummer morning, for instance at Midsummer the Sun rises directly over the Heel Stone at Stonehenge, England. Visit anywhere where there is a labyrinth, such as Glastonbury Tor. Go to gardens, walk and sit by ponds and lakes, or the sea itself, and watch the westering sun going down into the water. This is the time for large gatherings, parties, concerts, fetes, open-air plays. Morris Dances, which derive from older, Goddess-worshipping roots, are likely to be performed, so make a point of watching them. Think about all that brings you fulfilment and enjoyment.

Midsummer ritual

The cauldron is now filled with water and placed before the altar, wreathed in flowers. The altar itself is decorated with as many Summer blooms as possible. In Wiccan covens the drama of Oak King and Holly King is enacted by coven members, with Oak King giving way before his dark brother. The High Priest stands in the North and the High Priestess stands in front of him, holding a phallic wand, which may be a wand tipped with a pine cone. Holding the wand high, she says:

> *Great One of Heaven, Power of the Sun, we invoke thee in thine ancient names, Michael, Balin, Arthur, Lugh, Herne. Come again as of old into this thy land. Lift up thy shining spear of light to protect us. Put to flight the Powers of Darkness. Give us fair woodlands and green fields, blossoming orchards and ripening corn. Bring us to stand upon thy hill of Vision and show us the lovely realms of the gods.*

She traces the invoking pentagram before the High Priest who comes to her deosil and takes the wand with a kiss. Plunging it into the cauldron he says:

> *The spear to the cauldron, the lance to the grail, spirit to flesh, man to woman, sun to earth.*

The High Priestess sprinkles the coven with a heather branch, or similar, dipped in the cauldron, as they pass around the circle. She says:

> *Dance ye about the cauldron of Cerridwen the Goddess, and be ye blessed with the touch of this consecrated water, even as the sun, the Lord of Life, ariseth in his strength in the sign of the Waters of Life.*

(This is a reference to the astrological sign of Cancer, which the Sun enters at what is the Summer Solstice in the north.)

For your ritual you may like to have two candles, one for Oak King and one for Holly King, orange/red and dark green respectively. Place the cauldron so that the light of the candles is reflected in the water within, in the South of the circle. Reflect upon all that has brought you joy, and how that will change you, or enable you to make changes. When you are ready, extinguish the Oak King candle, saying, 'Farewell my Lord of Oak. May your journey to the silent and secret realms be peaceful. Go now, until we meet again.' Move the Holly King candle to stand now in the North, on the altar, and say, 'Well met my Lord of Holly. Guard the time of darkness, and may we grow in wisdom. Blessed Be.'

Light two more candles, preferably red ones, and place these on each side of the cauldron. Anoint each candle first with oil such as Ylang-ylang, or rosemary. Throw flowers of rose petals into the cauldron, as an offering, symbolic of the blessing of the Sun upon the land, and the waters and the bounty of the Goddess. Consecrate a special candle now to some project or cause, imbue it with power and light it from the candle to the West of the cauldron. Place it next to your Holly King candle. After your ritual move them both to a safe place and let them both burn out, naturally. Consecrate wine or orange juice and drink to the Great Mother and the Sun God at the height of His power. Call upon the Sun to bless the land:

> *Mighty Sun, lie warm upon the land, drawing forth peace and beauty. As your fiery chariot recedes into the mists of Otherworld, let your blessing remain in the fires of my spirit. Blessed Be.*

Walk slowly deosil around your circle, calling down the strength of the Sun, using your wand if you like. You may also incorporate the theme of the labyrinth into your ritual, by marking out a spiral with thread (a spiral may be considered another form of the labyrinth) which you tread, solemnly, to the centre. Meditate, and drink a toast. Close as usual, when ready.

LUGHNASADH

This festival is both a celebration of the harvest and a lament for the death of the Corn Spirit. Blood-red poppies stain the gold of the wheat fields, and the first touch of darkness is softly felt. And yet at the same time all is generosity, fruitfulness and plenty. The God is cut down and enters the Underworld but while the Goddess mourns, She also blesses. As Necessity, She is in a sense the hand that strikes Him, just as She, in season, gives back life. Many mythologies have stories of a dying and resurrecting god and this was mirrored in customs of sacrifice, such as the ritual slaying of the king, which is associated with several of the festivals. There is evidence that this happened in historical times, for example in the death of King Rufus, shot down in the New Forest at Lammas in 1100 CE, seemingly at his own behest.

The Earth mourns for the death that must be, in order for life to continue. However, this is merely metamorphosis, as the grain is transformed in loaves, and fruit becomes jams and pickles. Lugh is the name of a Celtic god of lightness and brightness, and while stories show Lugh Long-arm as master of craftsmanship and all the creative arts, his Welsh counterpart, Llew Llaw Gyffes, is cut down through the machinations of his wife, Blodeuwydd, who has been fashioned out of flowers (in true Nature Goddess style) and whose heart is as black as the midnight forest. Lughnasadh, which means the commemoration of Lugh, is also called Lammas or 'Loaf-mass'. You may wish to make some bread especially to form part of your ritual to celebrate the harvest. In times of old it was considered unlucky to be the one finally to fell the Corn Spirit, so the harvesters threw their sickles all together at the last stock. The best ears were then used to make a corn dolly.

Sacrifice is the theme at this time, and we may reflect that everything in life has a price. Really, this is not to be morose, but to realize in very truth that life depends on death. Sacrifices that we make are not for the purpose of self-abasement and self-hatred but in order that the greater spiritual self may grow. The changes presaged at Midsummer are beginning to show themselves, now, at Lughnasadh.

Things to do

In most places Lughnasadh occurs some days or weeks before the corn is cut (please note that by corn I mean wheat, not maize). If you go out and stand amid the corn you will feel the vibrant life of the corn and even sense a primal anger at its coming demise. The corn is whispering, watching, and there is a tragic, even fearful, presence amidst all the golden fertility. Small wonder that corn circles appear (although these are not only found in corn) in response possibly to this force. You may like to visit a crop circle, or even sleep out in one, to see what dreams and experiences arrive. You may like to go to a barn dance, or help with the harvest in some small way, where everything isn't totally mechanized. Make a corn dolly by twisting together ears of wheat and tying them in red ribbon – or make a really complex 'dolly' in a red skirt. Traditionally, the dolly was kept over the hearth and the seeds shaken out the following Spring, as part of the new sowing. Make bread also, for bread-making can be turned into a simple spell for peace and the growth of new life. This is the time for holidays, so take time out to consider your own personal 'harvest' in what you have done and also what you have given up to do it. Are you satisfied? Do you want this to continue?

Lughnasadh ritual

The altar can be decorated with first fruits, sheaves of corn, poppies and any other seasonal greenery and flowers. My choice now is for honey-coloured candles. A loaf should also be on the altar. In a Wiccan coven a chase similar to Beltane may be enacted, with the High Priest, as the God, laid low after his union with the Goddess, and covered with a green or brown cloth, as with a shroud. The High Priestess traces the invoking pentagram over the High Priest. Holding high the loaf she says:

> O mighty Mother of us all, Mother of all fruitfulness, give us fruit and grain, flocks and herds and children to the tribe that we may be mighty. By the rosy love do thou descend here upon thy servant and priestess.

She dances, holding the loaf, until she finishes her dance in front of the High Priest. The bread is broken and distributed to the coven as the Bread of Life, in order that 'sleep may lead to rebirth'. The 'shroud' is lifted from the High Priest as Holly King/Corn Spirit, who may then recite further verses of the 'Song of Amergin'. Janet and Stewart Farrar give this passage in *Eight Sabbats for Witches* (see Further Reading)

> I am a battle-waging spear;
> I am a salmon in the pool;
> I am a hill of poetry;
> I am a ruthless boar;
> I am a threatening noise of the sea;
> I am a wave of the sea;
> Who but I knows the secrets of the unhewn dolmen?

The High Priest is given a piece of the loaf by the High Priestess and after dancing and feasting the last of the loaf is returned to the earth.

For your ritual you may like to wear a red cord or scarf. Have two candles ready-lit on the altar with a third between them. Pass slowly deosil around your circle and face South, saying:

> Spread on the land the gold Sun lies,
> Sinks deep within, so sweetly dies

Then turn West with the words:

> Now dear life spent and poppies red
> Stain the flaxen Sun God's bed.

Turn now North, to the altar, and say:

> *So gather crops and brown bread rise*
> *See fresh, new-born life arise.*

Light the third candle. Take you red cord or scarf and knot it, thinking about any sacrifices you have made. Pass this over the candle, to encircle the base. Follow this, in the same way, with a green cord or cloth, to symbolize harvest and take a while to contemplate the meaning of 'harvest' and what it means to you. Consecrate a simple meal of bread and honey, offering this in consecration to the Four Quarters, feeling the gifts of each of the elements entering the food. Eat this in celebration, along with your consecrated wine and save some to give as an offering sandalwood to the earth, after your ritual. You might consecrate some sandalwood oil, in a carrier of wheatgerm oil (two drops per teaspoon) and anoint yourself, offering your strength to the Goddess and pledging perhaps a particular skill you have to be developed. You might consecrate some fruit in honour of your 'harvest' and fill your cauldron with it. Direct power towards it and eat some of it, keeping the rest to offer to friends and family. Give yourself whatever time you need to meditate and reflect. Close as usual when ready.

AUTUMN EQUINOX

At the Equinox the veil between this world and the next is thin, and hauntings are common because Otherworld comes close in the Autumn mists. Again we find ourselves on a threshold where light and dark are equal, but now dark is gaining. We are at the crossways, and the Autumn Equinox celebrates again the harvest, now gathered in, but also looks to the growth of darkness and the gaining of wisdom.

This was the time for the Eleusinian mysteries. The initiates were given the dictum, 'Know thyself'. Rites were designed to heighten and expand awareness, so that the mystery of life-in-death and death-in-life could be partaken of. At the climax of the ritual the initiate was shown a single ear of wheat with the words, 'In silence is the seed of wisdom gained'. The myth that formed the backdrop was that of Persephone/Kore and her abduction by the Underworld god Pluto or Dis. When Persephone was taken, her mother Demeter mourned unconsolably and, because Demeter was the Nature Goddess, the earth was plunged into Winter. The Olympian deities negotiated a compromise, where Persephone could return to her mother for part of the year, when Spring and Summer would reign, but when she returned as queen of the dark realms, Winter would come again. And so the seasonal cycle is set in motion. What Persephone actually undergoes, as we may understand it, is an initiation, a deep change, and her reality is no longer superficial. Although overtly patriarchal and brutal, Pluto may be an emissary of the Great Mother in some ways. She is changed by sexual love, which is the life force manifesting, and the earth changes with her.

This is a time for preserving and gathering, for husbanding resources and making best use of the remaining light and energy. It is also a time for turning inward – to 'know ourselves'.

Things to do

Make preserves and pickles, clear out cupboards in preparation for Winter. Plan to give yourself more 'dream time'. Take walks to look at the Autumn leaves, or go to an arboretum. Hold a 'harvest supper' for friends and family. Go blackberrying in a group, or on your own.

Autumn Equinox ritual

My choice for candles is blackberry purple. Blackberries, nuts, pine cones, acorns and similar can be placed on the altar along with an ear of wheat, on a special dish or lid. In a Wiccan ritual the coven are seated in a circle and the

137

covered dish is placed in the centre. The cover is lifted and the High Priestess says:

Behold the mystery: In silence is the seed of wisdom gained.

The group contemplate in silence. Then the High Priest stands in the West, the High Priestess in the East, facing each other, and she says:

> *Farewell, O Sun, ever-returning Light, the Hidden God, who ever yet remains, who now departs to the Land of Youth, through the Gates of Death, to dwell enthroned, the judge of Gods and men, the horned leader of the Hosts of Air. Yet even as He stands unseen about the circle, so dwelleth He within the secret seed, the seed of newly ripeneded grain, the seed of flesh hidden in the earth, the marvellous Seed of the Stars. In Him is Life and Life is the Light of man, that which was never born and never dies. Therefore the Wicca weep not, but rejoice.*

Now follows a dance, led by the High Priestess and High Priest, starting slowly and gaining speed, spiralling outwards. Feasting follows.

For your own ritual you may like to raise a cone of power and direct it towards any part of the globe that is suffering from famine. Fill your cauldron with ears of wheat, if you can, or place there your Lughnasadh corn dolly, or simply an ear of wheat that you uncover at a point in your rite, to contemplate. As this is a festival of wisdom, you may like to incorporate the number 7 in your observances, for example with seven candles, making seven circuits of the circle, or seven rings of the bell. Circle slowly around your cauldron at the centre of your circle, coming closer and closer to the centre. Contemplate your ear of wheat and light a candle, placing this in the cauldron with the words, 'May the flame of enlightenment, the inner fires of wisdom, be kindled all over the world.' While you may choose to move widdershins at certain points in your ritual, to mark the retreat of the year, the unwinding of life, trail a golden cord deosil around your cauldron, knotting it in the West with the words, 'The circle of life is unbroken, and eternal.' Keep the cord with your magical equipment, to place in an 'eternity' sign (a figure of eight on its side) around Spring flowers at your Spring Equinox rite, after which it may be returned to the earth. Make space in your Autumn Equinox ritual to consider both your personal 'harvest' and the things that have to go from your life, if that feels appropriate. For this you may use two small bowls of water, placing your finger in one and letting three drops fall into the other, naming these for three things that must change. Dispose of this is a stream, or the ocean, later, or simply pour out on the garden. Commune and close down as usual.

Study It will take some while to familiarize yourself with the meanings of the eight sabbats, so that they truly become part of you and so that their meanings expand and proliferate until you see them in almost everything. The sabbats are not merely an occasion for specific ritual but for all sorts of informal observance, activity and thought, some of which I have suggested. In addition there are many other myths and legends that have links with the sabbats, and you may discover or make up some of your own. This is both personal to you and a matter of collective worship, and these two strands interweave. Some books that you may find helpful: *The Wheel of the Year: Myth & Magic Through the Seasons*, Teresa Moorey and Jane Brideson (Hodder & Stoughton 1997), *A Calendar of Festivals*, Marian Green (Element 1991), *Eights Sabbats for Witches*, Janet and Stewart Farrar (Hale, 1989), *Hedgewitch*, Rae Beth (Hale, 1990). However, nothing can take the place of your own experience, feelings and actions, for witchcraft is not about learning with the head and thinking, but about doing, being and evolving.

TRAINING SESSION 6

Reflect   Think deeply about the next festival to come. What does it mean to you? What associations does it evoke, personally, generally, spiritually and physically? How does it make you feel, emotionally and in your body? What do you usually do at this time? What would you like to do? Where would you like to visit? Give some time to reflecting, trying to take the essence of the season deep into your bones and make a note of all images that arise in you. Always go for a walk near the time of the festival, whatever the weather may be.

Book of Shadows   Start a specific notebook for your observations on the year. For this you may use your Book of Shadows, but there may be too much material for that. Take a note of all your answers to the above, and also make a note if your mind is a 'blank' in any area.

Devise a ritual to celebrate the next sabbat, using as many or as few of the suggestions I have made as you wish. Draw on the suggested words and the Wiccan words, or compose your own. Do not worry if your ritual is very simple. Also, if you instinctively feel that something is appropriate but you are not sure why, go with your heart rather than your head. Note everything down in your Book of Shadows, for it is part of your growth. Make sure you actually perform your ritual. If time is short, or you are tired, tailor your ritual to match, because it is better to do what you can than overestimate and make too many demands on yourself, which can result in you doing nothing and feeling bad! The object of your observances are to draw you closer to the essence of Nature, of the Goddess and God, and to your own spiritual centre, in peace, beauty, love and celebration.

Note: The Wiccan information given in this chapter is drawn partly from my own records and topped up from Janet and Stewart Farrar's book, *Eight Sabbats for Witches* listed in Further Reading. For a full story, this work should be consulted.

7

THE MOON

Look for me by moonlight,
Watch for me by moonlight,
I'll come to thee by moonlight, though hell
  should bar the way.

ALFRED NOYES, *THE HIGHWAYMAN* (1906)

Every witch has a secret pact with the Moon, and in the monochrome of moonlight the witch shows her or his true colours. The Moon is the eye of the Goddess that sees into our souls, and Her white flames ignite the spirit. When the Full Moon shines like a gypsy's crystal, the past haunts, the future beckons and the present is transformed. Humans have learnt much from the Moon, and she stills offers her teachings, month by month.

These days the Moon isn't all she was, and poetry goes dry in the face of samples of lunar soil and plans to burn advertising symbols, by laser, onto her white face. We all know that the Moon is a lump of inert rock, and despite the way she glistens and gleams and hauls the tides around the earth, we know that there isn't a drop of water on her barren surface. And yet to de-sacralize the Moon is to complete the spiritual blood-sucking that has turned us into 'ghosts in the machinery' and to forget that the material world is a metaphor for spirit. Through the bright portal of the Moon shines the light of Otherworld, and hers is the touch of magic. We need to learn to look at the Moon as our ancestors did, and remember.

THE MOON IS HISTORY

The Moon's promise of renewal was not lost upon Stone Age people, and it may have been from observation of the Moon that we learnt to think in the abstract, able to hold in our minds an idea, a belief, even when the external testimony had disappeared. By waxing, becoming full, waning and disappearing, only to reappear once more, the message of the Moon was 'out of sight, but *not* out of mind'! As the Moon was regularly reborn, so humans could hope to be born again. The sacred mounds in which the dead were buried often faced eastwards, to the moonrise, so that the souls of the departed might ride home one the moonbeams. In her alternating darkness and light the Moon encodes the all-containing Goddess, her patterns enshrining the paradox of life that must include death.

In most cultures mythology associated with the Moon predates by centuries that associated with the Sun. Stone Age artfacts convey many samples of awareness of lunar phases, and a well-known example is that of the Goddess of Willendorf, on whose 20,000-year-old head are notched seven layers of circles, which probably relate to the interval of approximately seven days between each of the Moon's quarters. As the days of the hunter-gatherers gave way to the development of agriculture, the links of the Moon with more of life's mysteries became evident, for the waxing, full and waning Moon mirrors the passage of a seed, from dormancy, through growth, bloom, decay and return of seed to soil. In *Cities of Dreams* by Stan Gooch, discussed earlier (and listed in Further Reading), Neanderthal peoples are described as being nocturnal, worshipping the Moon and having a strongly magical consciousness. Certainly the internal atmosphere evoked by the Moon speaks of an ancestral dream time and of a oneness – knowledge that we have largely lost. This consciousness is important to witches

THE MOON AND THE GODDESS
■

The Moon resonates with the concept of the Goddess. When the waxing sliver appears in the rosy evening, this seems to relate naturally to the Maiden; the egg-like orb of Full Moon, queening it at midnight, relates to the Mother; and the waning crescent, spotted in the dawn by insomniacs, relates to the Crone. Now the Moon is lost to the night sky for several days, until her rebirth again as Maiden. The dark of the moon may be related to the Goddess, Present and Unseen. In all her characteristics, of cyclicity, relationship with times of day when the unconscious and the instincts hold sway, in sexual activity and dreams, in her reflective nature, her lack of stridency, and her beauty, the Moon strikes us as feminine. However, it is important to remember that there were many Moon gods in ancient cultures. The notion of the Moon as the 'other husband' of women was widespread, and some believed that it was the Moon who made women pregnant. Our identification of the Moon with feminity and the Goddess may say a great deal about our culture. However, we may grow close to the Moon in goddesses such as Celtic Bride and Graeco-Roman Artemis/ Diana, while Hecate is our Dark Moon guide.

There are those who argue that to assign the Moon as feminine and the Sun as masculine is to demean the status of women, leaving them passive and relatively powerless. Indeed, why should not the Feminine blaze out, bright as the Sun? Why should the Masculine not identify with the gentle and instinctual? Janet McCrickard puts forward powerful evidence and argument for the Sun as feminine, in *Eclipse of the Sun* (see Further Reading) However, I still prefer the Moon as Goddess, for the following reasons. Firstly, the earth seems unarguably our 'mother' in that she nurtures us and maintains our life. Earth and Moon are a system, for the Moon is a large satellite, and to imagine that the Moon orbits a static Earth is false, for the Moon's gravity is strong enough to cause the Earth also to orbit the Moon, although to a much lesser degree. The Moon rules the tides, and the watery medium does seem linked to the Feminine. For me the Moon is the Earth's celestial counterpart, the Goddess-in-the-sky, her rhythms being the same as women's rhythms, while the solar rhythms are more extended and more radical. The Moon seems to exemplify all that we need to redeem in ourselves, our instincts, our sense of natural rhythms, our ability to be non-invasive, to attune rather than to subdue, to look inwards rather than judging what is external to us, to redevelop our psychic and intuitional faculties and to dissolve boundaries rather than erect and maintain them. Currently women are indeed finding 'liberation' and they are able to express themselves and compete in the neon light and concrete structure of our cultures. Despite that prevailing 'glass ceiling' women are asserting their freedom to be as men with ever-growing power. However, it is debatable whether they are any more free to be women, or to explore what that may mean. Nor are men sufficiently free to explore their gentler qualities. To me the Moon seems to represent adequately what we need to redeem, in deity and in ourselves, and that is largely about feminity. However, in this as in all else, you are free to form your own associations and concepts. Let the moonlight awaken you.

THE PHASES OF THE MOON

Astronomically, the phases of the Moon are due to the inter-relationship of the Earth, Sun and Moon. The changing shape of the Moon is due to the different way the light from the sun is reflected by the Moon, not, of course, through any actual change in the shape of the Moon. So does that mean that lunar phases don't really matter, because it's actually always the same old Moon, anyway? Not at all! It is how we perceive it that is the crux of the

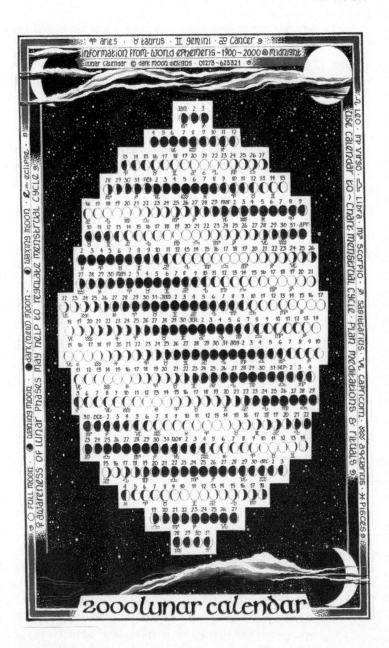

The lunar calendar

matter. I once read a book about magic, which argued that the phrases aren't important and that you don't have to take note of them in your rites, because even if the Moon is waning here, then another Moon, going around another planet somewhere in the universe, is waxing! That amazed me, because we are not on that planet, looking at that Moon, but on this one, and one of the bases of witchcraft is the sense of 'nowness' and attunement to the prevailing tides here, not light years away. Understanding of the phases is useful, but that should hopefully not prevent you getting into the 'feel' of them.

New Moon refers to the time when the Moon reappears in the evening sky, moving, in effect, away from the Sun. The crescent is now growing, as the waxing Moon. In the northern hemisphere the shape of the waxing crescent is imitated by a raised, cupped right hand; the waning crescent by a left hand, and this is reversed in the southern hemisphere. However, the phases are the same over the entire globe: a waxing Moon in the North is a waxing Moon in Australia; Full Moon is Full Moon everywhere, although naturally the Moon is in the sky at different times at different places when viewed from Earth. The crescent fills out until it becomes a perfect orb at Full Moon, and wears away again, as the Moon rises later and later. The waning crescent disappears in the dawn sky. The three or four days when the Moon is invisible, because she is close to the Sun, are called Dark-of-the-Moon.

There is some misunderstanding of lunar phases and cycles, and they are often confused with the time taken by the Moon to pass through the zodiac. The Moon takes approximately 29$\frac{1}{2}$ days to pass from Full Moon to Full Moon again. However, it takes slightly less than 28 days to pass through all the signs of the zodiac, from the start of Aries back again to the start of the sign. It is often said that there are 13 lunar months in the year, which is more or less correct for the zodiac cycle (13 × 28 = 364) but that does not mean that there are 13 Full Moons in a year. There *may* be in some years. Most years have 13 New Moons or 13 Full Moons, but never both (because $29^1/_2 \times 13 = 383^1/_2$ and there are only 365 days in a year) and some years miss out altogether and only have twelve of each phase. The Moon has caused conundrums for calendar-makers. Nonetheless, 13 months of 28 days each would be a lot neater than the present system which sticks to the clumsy division by 12. However, 12 is a neater number to a rational consciousness, and the ejection of the Moon from our calendar has a lot to say about solar, patriarchal takeover. Nonetheless, the word month derives from Moon, as do many other words, such as *measurement, commensurate* and *dimension*. It was from the Moon that the first notion of measuring came.

Another phenomenon that is of interest to witches, astrologers and others is that of eclipses. A solar eclipse is caused when the Moon comes between the Sun and the Earth, and a lunar eclipse when the Earth comes between the Sun and the Moon. Not all eclipses are total, for these depend on exact alignments and correct distances, which are astronomically variable. An eclipse of the Sun is followed by an eclipse of the Moon, roughly six months later. Solar eclipses can only occur at New Moon, lunar eclipses at Full Moon, and while a solar eclipse can only last for up to eight minutes, the Full Moon may be eclipsed for two hours and is visible over the entire night hemisphere, while a solar eclipse is only visible over a portion of the daylight globe.

Opinions vary concerning eclipses. They were certainly considered fateful in past times, when a solar eclipse foretold the death of the sovereign. Astrologers generally regard them as times of intensity, or 'wipe-out', when Sun and Moon are in especially powerful conjunction (solar eclipse) or opposition (lunar eclipse), and an astrological chart drawn up for the time of an eclipse can resonate with national and political affairs. Eclipses are not generally specifically celebrated by witches, but will be noted by them as affecting the tides of life. Many may wish to abstain from magical activity, or only concentrate on specific matters at times of eclipse. The significance of eclipses is something you may like to explore, with reference to your own reactions, and if you have your birth chart, and possess some knowledge of astrology, you will find it relevant to note what contacts the point of the eclipse makes in your own chart. Generally speaking, the highly charged eclipse times are not favoured for ordinary rituals, but for more inward work.

Regarding the observable effects of the lunar phases, opinions vary, and while there is documentation regarding the rise of crime, incidence of admission to mental institutions, and haemorrhage on the operating table, associated with Full Moon, there are those who assert that there is no hard evidence that Full Moon has any effect. Sexual activity of humans and animals seem to increase at Full Moon. Seeds planted at a waxing Moon have a better rate of germination than those planted when she is waning, as I have proved by trial and error. My midwife recently told me that they know to expect more births as the moon rises to full, showing the pragmatic and time-honoured wisdom of those who are close to life's momentous passages! Oysters brought inland have been shown to adapt their opening and closing in direct response to the moon overhead. Our bodies, being some two-thirds water, might be thought to resonate to the Moon, as do the tides. The most obvious link with human life that the Moon evinces connects to menstruation, which we shall be looking at more closely. Exposure to the light of Full Moon has been thought to help infertile women conceive, and pregnancy, which we are told lasts 40 weeks, takes nine Moons (i.e. $9 \times 29\frac{1}{2}$ days) from conception to birth, so babies who are born at term arrive at the same phase as their conception.

MENSTRUATION
■

The liberation of women has meant the liberation of menstruation. We no longer have to suffer in silence, but can complain openly about 'the curse'. What we do not do is value our periods. We see them as an interference in life: messy, painful and a nuisance, resenting them as a barrier placed upon us, as women, when we are determined to be 'equal'. In so doing we actually sell out pretty thoroughly to patriarchal values. (Guys, please bear with us here, for this section is of relevance and interest to male witches. For centuries women have studied the feelings and reactions of people, especially the all-powerful male, and if you want to catch up with us in the wisdom this affords, now is your chance!)

A woman's menstrual cycle is more than mere biology, for it gives women their diversity, their creativity and their 'witchiness'. Through the month a woman has a chance to explore several different facets of her being. Because cultural norms demand that we remain pretty much the same, operating to a routine, we have to struggle against our inner tides. Most jobs and schedules are compatible with masculine, linear consciousness, so it is no wonder that a woman gets pre-menstrual syndrome (PMS) when she has to struggle with cars and trains, computers and ledgers, cooking and washing, at times when she really needs to take notice of her hormonal signal to retreat, meditate and create inwardly. Women might be better served by a routine that allows them to work with greater intensity at some times of the month, when energy is at its height, and to recharge at others.

It is when a women is ovulating that her attunement is most in harmony with prevailing patriarchal attitudes, for she is likely to be more acquiescent, more receptive to sexual advance, but also more energetic and outwardly positive. This fertile time is naturally valued as a time when

149

a child may be conceived. Conversely, when a woman has her period, it is the time of the birth of the 'magical child' when no human conception is likely to be possible. At this time women are more likely to be divergent, rebellious, individual, and much less biddable. It isn't hard to see how this appears threatening to a patriarchal consciousness, and because of this the Bible gives rules concerning the uncleanliness of menstrual blood. Menstruation is the time when life can be seen not to exist in the bleeding womb. The blood becomes linked to the cannibalism of babies and destructive to 'common decency'. Most of us would never put it that way today, but yet if you really think about it, the attitudes are there. But what is so repulsive about menstrual blood? Its beautiful colour, like best Burgundy, is a testament of each woman's creativity, on so many levels. Straining against the requirements of a period must be the greatest single cause of PMS.

Menstruation is in a sense an initiation, a descent into one's inner world, and the 'wise wound' of the period may be a gateway to spirit flight, shamanic revelation and inspiration of all sorts. Women have a special power at the time of their period because they may be in closer contact with their unconscious. Some of the 'bad temper' displayed at this time is very likely to be because the unconscious isn't being listened to. It was probably a recognition of the power inherent in the period, rather than a rejection of the woman as 'unclean', that lay behind tribal customs of segregation. Secret fascination and desire for this blood may lie behind vampire tales and other folklore. For instance, the novel and film *The Exorcist* (1973) can be seen as a symbolic exploration of the menarche (the first occurrence of menstruation in a woman's life), which is personified as a repulsive and horrifying demon. Most cultures have a myth that in some long-distant time men stole power from women, symbolising the repression of menstrual potentials and needs, while circumcision at puberty may be a way to emulate the menarche.

The adoption of a menstrual cycle, as opposed to an oestrus cycle, by the human female has had an immense effect on our society, as it provides opportunity for more lasting relationships and an extended spectrum of sexual expression. Because the human female is potentially receptive to sexual advance at all times, sexuality has been separated from procreation, as an expression of love. Of course, this also means that a woman may say 'no' and this has enormous implications for relationships, which require subtlety, understanding and responsiveness.

We have already noted the links between the Moon and menstruation, but these are often quite specific. Many women menstruate at New Moon, and many at Full Moon. New Moon menstruation may mean a woman can follow the Moon, through waxing, full and waning, experiencing the potential and awakening of the Maiden at New, the Mother's creativity at Full, the Crone's wisdom when waning and the mysteries of the Goddess, Present and Unseen at Dark Moon, when the period arrives and the woman 'rebirths' herself. Others who menstruate at Full Moon may be regarded as having the 'Wise Woman' cycle. Creativity may be heightened at Dark Moon, while the Full Moon throws into relief the inner qualities at menstruation. Others, of course, do not have nearly so regular a cycle, nor does a woman's cycle necessarily span 29 days. However, if the phases of the Moon are noted, they are usually found to have an effect, the period perhaps coming earlier or late to align with New or Full Moon, in each individual. Observation of the Moon in relation to periods has been known to regulate a haphazard cycle, and taking note of and respecting the cycle and its nuances may mean an easier passage into menopause, when a woman holds all the wisdom of the menstruating years, deepening inside her body. However, women who have gone through the menopause or a hysterectomy may still discern a cycle within, relating to the Moon, and this can be a help in attuning to the requirements of the body and the spirit. All these remarks are intended to invite interest, reflection and observation, not as final definitions, for each woman's cycle is her own. The pity of it is that we generally take so little notice of it.

While men do not menstruate, they are cyclical even so. Men are especially apt to believe they should be constant, consistent, always energetic, always achieving. It is far kinder to the guys to recognize that a cycle is indeed in process, and to take note of the phases of the Moon to see if you can understand this. Naturally this is much harder for a man, for his cycles are far less well-defined, and the ability of many men to tune into this instinctual panorama needs a lot of encouragement before it begins to be effective. Men who have female partners may like to learn from their partner's ebb and flow, and so find attunement to their own. Men who do not have a female partner can still find all the help they need in the Moon. In making contact with the inner Feminine or anima, the Moon can show men the way, dropping hints, attuning them to the tides of their soul. This is achieved in no logical way, but happens, by regularly noting the lunar phases and sitting or walking in the moonlight. Many men will find that they are most energetic at Full Moon, but this isn't always so, and there are grounds for believing that men adapt to the rhythms of their partners, so having greatest energy and sexuality when the partner is ovulating. Of course, not all women experience greatest energy when ovulating. For some this may occur at the time of the period. These are subtle and individual matters, found by observation and experimentation, there to be creatively adapted and used magically, and presided over by the Moon.

MOON MAGIC

We 'know' the Moon is magical, and in some ways it seems a shame to unpack this. However, no words can ever catch a moonbeam, or find the way to the recesses of your heart, so easily fingered by moonlight. The moon is magical because she awakens the instinctual Self, and this Self is at once an ancient, fork-tongued reptile and a dancing elf, blithe with eternal youth. The Moon will teach you, wordlessly, if you will only observe and listen with your inner ear.

Specifically, the phases of the Moon are related to magic, in that we can use a time when the Moon is waxing or full for most magic, certainly anything that relates to increase, creativity and progress.

If we wished to get rid of something, say a wart, then we would probably choose the time when the Moon is waning, for as the Moon wanes, so we could expect the wart to 'wane'. Sometimes the right seasonal festivals are celebrated at the nearest Full Moon to the festival, rather than on the date, and Samhain might be celebrated at Dark Moon. As you become more acquainted with the lunar phases and how they affect you, you may find it best to adapt your activity to some extent to the Moon, beginning tasks as the Moon waxes, bringing them to fruition at Full Moon and winding down as she wanes, using Dark Moon to retreat. Of course this is usually not possible to any great extent, but if you can make changes and you feel these would help, that is part of living magically.

Witches celebrate Full Moon at a festival called an 'esbat', although many witches these days do not have time for specific workings, and have their hands full concentrating on the eight sabbats. Full Moon is a time for all magical workings and is generally less specific than the sabbats. One major part of an esbat may be the 'drawing down of the Moon' upon a priestess, so that she embodies the Goddess to the others present, and herself experiences a great expansion of vision. This is also a way of honouring the Goddess and the Moon. Drawing down the Moon is also part of the sabbat ceremony for Wiccans. The High Priest draws down the Moon upon the High Priestess, as she stands with her back to the altar, in the Osiris-risen position. Firstly he gives her the 'five fold kiss' which means he kisses her feet, knees, womb, breasts and lips, in that order, saying:

> *Blessed be thy feet that have brought thee in these ways*
> *Blessed be thy knees that have knelt at the sacred altar*
> *Blessed be thy womb, without which we would not be*
> *Blessed be thy breasts, formed in perfect beauty*
> *Blessed be thy lips that shall utter the Sacred Names.*

They embrace, the High Priest kneels again and continues:

> *I invoke thee and call upon thee, Mighty Mother of us all, bringer of all fruitfulness; by seed and root, by bud and stem, by leaf and flower and fruit, by life and love do I invoke thee to descend upon the body of this thy servant and priestess.*

As he says this he touches her in turn upon her breasts and womb, twice. Still kneeling he continues:

> *Hail, Aradia! From the Amalthean Horn*
> *Pour forth thy store of love; I lowly bend*
> *Before thee, I adore thee to the end*
> *With loving sacrifice thy shrine adorn*
> *Thy foot is to my lip (as he kisses her right foot)*
> *My prayer upborn*
> *Upon the rising incense-smoke; then spend*
> *Thine ancient love, O Mighty One, descend*
> *To aid me, who without thee am forlorn.*

Now he stands up and takes a step backwards, and the High Priestess draws the Earth-invoking pentagram in the air before him with the wand, saying:

> *Of the Mother darksome and divine*
> *Mine the scourge and mine the kiss*
> *The five-point star of love and bliss –*
> *Here I charge you, in this sign.*

Now the Moon has been drawn down, and the Great Mother Charge follows, as given in Chapter 2.

In *West Country Wicca* (see Further Reading) Rhiannon Ryall says that at the Full Moon ceremony a large shallow dish was placed in the circle to reflect the Moon, and that the Moon could only be drawn down upon a woman who was 'fully woman', that is not a maid. It was always drawn down upon a woman of child-bearing age, as she represented fertile potential, and it was considered best if she were menstruating at the time, so emphasizing her feminity. The ceremony was much simpler, the High Priestess standing with the dish of water at her feet, and the High Priest saying:

> O Gracious Goddess, behold thy priestess ... [name],
> Bring down thy power upon her and within her,
> That through thy Great Art she may see those things
> Which are hidden, and know thy wisdoms which she
>   lacks.
> O Lady of the Fields, enter now thy Priestess ... [name].

The Moon was not drawn down in the Winter months, as these were given over to God, while the Lady slept. Rhiannon Ryall makes the further point that when the experience of drawing down is complete, one is in a transcendent state, and so it would hardly be possible to recite the Charge. However, the Charge tends to come out slightly differently everytime, modified by the trance-like state. It is true that simpler rituals and greater spontaneity may make for deeper experience, and you may have a vivid and inspiring drawing down quite on your own, with no words at all. The purpose of drawing down the Moon is to enhance our experience of other realms and receive insight, and to bring power into the circle. It is also an act of worship of the Goddess.

To draw down the Moon alone you may simply stand before your cauldron, or dish, or hold your chalice and say something like:

Great Goddess, bright lady, come into my soul
Let your wisdom be mine, let your power fill me
May my being shine with your light
That has guided the ancients, down the ages
Filling the heart with blessed hunger
And bringing a fulfilment beyond imagining
Be within me now
Great Goddess
Aradia, Diana, Levannah
Isis, Selene, Astarte
Be within me now.

However, you may draw down the Moon with no words, and I find that I say whatever comes into my head, while my mind travels through the oceans, and across the star-lit sky. This is a wonderful experience. However, I think it is best to wait until you feel ready to do this, after you have completed your initial training and been initiated, or have initiated yourself. Make sure that you ground yourself thoroughly after you come back to Earth.

THE MOON AND THE CIRCLE

We have seen how the circle is quartered in relation to the four elements and directions, and how the Wheel of the Year can also be shown, each of the eight sabbats having their place. Lunar phases also take their place on this mandala, with Dark Moon and all its associations with the Unseen Goddess placed at the North with Earth (in the southern hemisphere you may choose to place this in the South), the waxing Moon in the East with Air as the Maiden Goddess, the Full Moon in the South with Fire as the creativity of the Mother Goddess (North, for the southern hemisphere), and the Waning Moon in the West with Water and the counsel of the Crone. Thus the four phases of the Moon are another metaphor for inner balance. Observing the phases can lead us to hidden parts of ourselves. For instance, a woman may find that her 'inferior' function (as described in Chapter 4) is more in evidence when she is menstruating, in contact with her unconscious, and this may correlate with Dark or Full Moon. Simply by watching our own ebb and flow we can discover much about ourselves.

Lunar observance In a notebook, start to make notes about your feelings and impressions, your health and vitality, your creativity, dreams, preferences, thoughts and opinions, through the phases of the Moon. Note what you do, and how you do it, not in a spirit of 'and then this happened, and then that', but in terms of what was going on for you. Try not to be too analytical, just be aware. If you find this a strain then simply write down what occurs. Do this for at least three months, preferably six, and see if you can discern a pattern to your activities and feelings, related to the Moon.

Decide to celebrate the phases of the Moon in daily life. At Full Moon you may like to light a candle, drink some wine, throw a party; at Dark Moon you may like to meditate, practise astral travel or shamanic journeying.

Make an altar to the Moon on a shelf or space in your home. Place there anything that appeals: shells, precious stones, goddess-figures, silver artefacts (silver is considered to be ruled by the Moon), animal figures such as dogs, wolves, dolphins, snakes, or any other figures or symbols that seem appropriate. Stones ruled by the Moon are quartz, pearl, moonstone, crystal, sapphire, selenite, mother-of-pearl, chalcedony, beryl, aquamarine. However, you might like to try alternate stones, choosing different ones for varying phases. And you might like to depart from the traditional associations, placing ruby, garnets or other red stones on your altar at Full Moon and black stones such as onyx or apache tear there at Dark Moon. An image draped in dark cloth would represent the Goddess, Present and Unseen at Dark Moon. Cards and calendars can be obtained from Dark Moon Designs (see Resources), and one way to represent the four phases immediately and evocatively is to place the appropriate card for the phase on your altar. Light candles on your altar or mark the phases as you wish. If you are a menstruating woman you may wish to mark this in some way upon your lunar altar, perhaps by placing there a red stone, and you may celebrate it subtly by wearing a red scarf, too. The Lunar Calendar by Dark Moon Designs has space to colour in the phases, as you menstruate. If you no longer menstruate, or if you are a man, the Moon is equally your friend, so celebrate the cyclicity that you discover within on your altar.

Menstrual mandala Female witches will find that their awareness of the tides of their own power is greatly increased by the construction of a menstrual mandala. To do this you can draw a large circle on a piece of plain paper and divide it into the days of your period. I have always found it difficult to divide into 29, but if you roughly quarter it, leaving one quarter slightly larger, and divide three quarters into seven and one into eight, this can be achieved. Naturally if your cycle is a different length you can divide the circle accordingly. Draw the phases of the Moon around your circle and divide each section to give space to dreams, feelings and moods, mental acuity, physical sensations, sexual desire and activity, creativity, etc., obviously noting the days when you menstruate.

Dreams are most important, and it is best to keep a dream diary, in as much detail as time will allow. Please do not attempt too much, or you will probably give up after a week or two. Noting dreams is a way of attuning to your unconscious. Dreams may be inspirational, even prophetic. Certainly they are a clue as to what is going on deep inside. Try not to be literal about dreams and their symbols, striving for a pat and detailed interpretation. Sometimes it is best to stay with the feeling that it was an important dream, rather than to spell out what it meant, for in that way some things may be lost.

Back to your mandala. If your cycle is irregular, continue around the perimeter, in a spiral, if necessary. Use different colours, if you wish, for different matters. The use of the circular design, or mandala, is symbolic of wholeness. Start at the top and plot the colours in a clockwise direction. After doing this for a few months you will begin to get a total picture of your cycle and yourself, able to recall different times of the month with more clarity, less surprised by your moods and generally more connected to bits of you that are often repressed.

Remember that your period is a time when you may be very magically powerful and when states of trance may be more accessible to you. If you are a man you may still like to plot the phases of the Moon in a circle and record your reactions and feelings.

The Moon in the signs of the Zodiac   In my opinion, the phase of the Moon is more important magically than its entry into the signs of the Zodiac. However, these too are significant. If you wish to apply them to your observations and workings you will need some planetary tables (called an Ephemeris) which should be obtainable in most large bookshops, and if not can be ordered. You will also need knowledge of symbols, because the Ephemeris will use these. The glyph for the Moon is ☽ and for each of the signs ♈ ARIES, ♉ TAURUS, ♊ GEMINI, ♋ CANCER, ♌ LEO, ♍ VIRGO, ♎ LIBRA, ♏ SCORPIO, ♐ SAGITTARIUS, ♑ CAPRICORN, ♒ AQUARIUS, ♓ PISCES.

Generally speaking, when the Moon is in Aries, this is good for anything dynamic, assertive, bold, new enterprise, adventure, risk-taking, decision-making, but watch out for impulsiveness and for things being short-lived. Aries is Cardinal Fire. In Taurus, construction and solidity are highlighted, also concerns to do with money and sexual love, and the home. This is not a good time for changes. What you start may last, even if you'd prefer otherwise! Taurus is Fixed Earth. Gemini is quick, witty and very changeable. A good time for communication and exchange of ideas, also for playfulness. Gemini is Mutable Air. Moon in Cancer is a sensitive time, when the Moon is in her own sign. Workings to do with home and family, but be careful not to upset anyone. Full Moon in Cancer may be especially magical, and a time for important dreams. Cancer is Cardinal Water. Leo relates to the creative and dramatic, entertainment and showmanship. Good for workings related to these and also for self-expression, vitality and a more subtle but powerful sense of individuality and will. However, keep a sense of proportion. Leo is Fixed Fire. Moon in Virgo highlights details, precision, routine and research, also health. Virgo is Mutable Earth. Libra is Cardinal Air and related to social graces, diplomacy, charm, artistic expression and partnerships in marriage, business or friendship, so now is a good time to work for these. Scorpio, sign of Fixed Water, relates to the unconscious, powerful sexual drives, passions and much that is hidden. Use this time with care! Moon in the Mutable Fire sign of Sagittarius is good for philosophy, higher education, imagination and generally opening up to new ideas and adventures. Capricorn, sign of Cardinal Earth, relates to the establishment, authority figures, professional advancement, hard work and discipline. There may be obstacles. Regulations and practicality are important. Moon in Aquarius relates to anything futuristic, individual, quirky, intellectual, humanitarian and idealistic, but don't get too detached. Aquarius is Fixed Air. Lastly to Pisces and Mutable Water, a time for all that is spiritual, dreamy, mystical, foretelling the future or developing psychism. There may also be confusion, escapism, manipulation, so be wary of these.

If the Moon's zodiacal position is taken into account, this should be in conjunction with lunar phases. For instance, a New Moon in Aries would be especially good for fresh enterprise, while the Full Moon in Cancer highlights creativity, pregnancy etc. Remember that when the Moon is very new it is still in 'conjunction' with the Sun, which will result in an extreme emphasis on the sign in question, which could be overpowering. Also when the Moon is Full, the Sun is opposite it, implying balance and also incorporating the characteristics of the Sun-sign.

Thus Full Moon in Cancer means Sun in Capricorn, so practicality is favoured. These factors can become quite complex and to incorporate them fully will require some study. It is up to you how far you wish to go. Some knowledge and understanding of the phases is essential, I believe, but further study is optional.

8

POWER AND MAGIC

Knowledge is power.

SEVENTEENTH-*CENTURY PROVERB*

WHAT IS WITCHCRAFT?

Perhaps the best and most often-quoted definition of magic is that of Aleister Crowley. Magic is 'the Science and Art of causing Change to occur in conformity with the Will'. You may say, with some justification, that you do that every time you lift your mug and take a sip of coffee. You cause a change in the cup and its contents, and in your body's metabolism. This is true, but Crowley's definition rests on more specific meanings. For instance, I think we may take Crowley to mean by 'Will' something more than our everyday whims and desire, and 'Change' to be something more fundamental. The 'art of causing change' is not commonly found, for we tend to go through life automatically, reacting to stimuli from others and from the environment, rather than consciously structuring our lives. We live according to internalized 'scripts', such as 'Nothing good ever happens to me', or the milder but more insidious 'I'm just average'. Reforming such an outlook is indeed a far-reaching change, and connects to another quotation from Dion Fortune: 'Magic is the art of changing consciousness at will'. Changing consciousness is an enormous undertaking, and if we do it successfully, life definitely does change. Furthermore, as we draw closer to our centre, we become more in tune with our 'true will' which is about our essence, our purpose, the part of us closest to the Goddess and the God, not the desires of the ego.

Anyone who succeeds in making a real change in their lives, a real shift in vision, has in a way worked an act of magic. Once consciousness changes, something alchemical goes to work in life and outward changes follow. Some of these can be seen as natural reactions of other people to our different approach, but there is more to it than that, for things that are appropriate to our new life path are mysteriously drawn to out fresh magnetism. This is one of the reasons why self-understanding is so necessary to the magical practitioner. Most of this is generally acceptable to people interested in personal growth, and only brushes against metaphysics. But is magic real? By our spells, our visualization and our willpower, do we set a real force in motion? The answer is yes.

The reality that we see is only a very small part of the true picture, for all of existence is energy at different rates of vibration. Our material world is on the densest, slowest vibrational rate, and because of this, magical effects are not witnessed dramatically, for the changes that we intend, and the way in which we all structure our own lives by our thoughts, comes about after a time-lag. The old saying, 'As you think, so you become' proves itself slowly and in non-obvious ways. Occultists tell us that, in contrast, on the astral plane, or the next vibrational rate, change manifests itself instantly. When we perform a magical working we are, in a sense, creating a template on the astral, into which material events gradually shape themselves, hopefully!

All matter can be perceived as different vibrational rates along a spectrum, and this could be part of the logic behind all of the props we use for spells and magic – that these articles resonate with 'higher' levels. (Please note, I have placed 'higher' in inverted commas, because no vibrational rate is really better or more spiritual. The material world isn't a base den of iniquity but a place designed for specific purposes, experiences and learning.) However, witches don't really analyse this, it just 'feels right' to use certain things and certain colours. When you are in any doubt, go with what feels right for you.

SCIENCE AND MAGIC

The received wisdom of science is inimical to witchcraft, and has, in fact, taken over from fundamental monotheism as the current dogma. Scientists cannot be effectively challenged, unless you have a doctorate in the subject, and then you have probably 'sold out' along the way to accepted values. Scientists are very proud of the way they are 'objective' and deal in 'the facts'. However, history demonstrates inexorably that what was once considered proven hard fact gives way to new material, and the ultimate pinnacle of knowledge of 100 years ago is now laughable. Rest assured, 100 or 200 years from now, much that we take as gospel will be regarded the same way. This is not to say that science is useless, for of course it is not. Science is about the observed and the workable. We need always to bear in mind that there may be things we have overlooked, or that could work better. Many scientists are reluctant to change their views and again history is full of examples of brilliant men who were squashed by their peers, and of important data that was left out of the picture because it didn't fit in with the theories of some esteemed doctor. Another little foible of scientists, being largely 'thinking types' (see Chapter 4), is that their emotions may be unacknowledged. In the worst scenario this may result in some cherished theory being guarded by a jealous and powerful intellect with all the savagery of a lion guarding its cub, the emotional need to be 'right' quite unrecognized and concealed by a barrage of logic.

I do not mean to denigrate science, for without it I could not bash away at this keyboard in comfortable surroundings even though outside is a grey, October morning. However, in my view science is to be used and adapted, not 'believed' in'. The best example I know concerning how we see what we believe is that of the South American natives who *could not see* the large, ocean-going vessels that brought the Europeans to them, and marvelled that they could appear from the ocean in such small boats! The natives did not believe ocean-going boats were possible, thus to them they were invisible. Can we dismiss this as the confined consciousness of primitive natives? I think not! How do we know just how much we are not seeing? Is it not worthwhile, at least, to keep an open mind?

As far as I am aware, there are many complex systems that science cannot map, for instance the motion of the waterwheel. Such systems may be thrown out by the incursion of very small stimuli. This has given rise to 'chaos theory' with the intriguing idea that the flutter of a butterfly's wings over America might cause a hurricane in Hong Kong. This can fuel our outrage at the tinkering with the biosphere that is arrogantly pursued by agro-business and its employed scientific staff, the worst of all being genetic engineering. We cannot possibly predict what will happen if the 'gene-ies' really get their way, and while we may be blandly reassured by some white-coated PR person, we know that the underlying motives are profit and power. However, here I digress into the realms of politics, in which some witches may be active, but this is outside our scope here. Suffice to say that chaos theory is not inimical to magic, for if the random flutter of insects' wings can achieve so much, what might the concentrated magical practitioner do with the power of ritual?

Some enlightened scientists certainly do veer almost towards a spiritual viewpoint. For instance, earlier this century the astronomer James Jeans stated that 'The Universe begins to look more like a great thought than a great machine'. C.G. Jung developed his theory of synchronicity, in which he argued that meaningful connections can exist between events that are other than cause and effect. This sounds magical to me. More recently, the biologist Rupert Sheldrake, in his book *The Hypothesis of Formative Causation*, (see Further Reading) put forward his theory of morphogenetic fields, which are a non-physical patterning existing behind physical form. The 'morphic resonance' existing in these fields gives the individual access to sources of information located outside the physical brain, such as species memory. In this way, a seed knows how to become a plant, an egg knows how to become a bird, ovum and sperm know how to make a human. Further than this, quantum physics indicates that the mind of the observer has an effect on the process of an experiment (no surprise to your average witch). An example is given by the process of shining a beam of light through a pinhole, to appear on a screen. If two pinholes are present and the beams cross, the crossover point will have several dark lines, where the photons interfere with each other, and cancel each other out. If the beam is subsequently dimmed so that only a single photon can pass through at a time, these lines ought to disappear, because one photon cannot interfere with another. However, if these beams are applied to a photographic plate, interference lines are still present. Yet if the photons are watched with a photon detector, the pattern of interference disappears. (These and similar matters are more fully described by writers such as Colin Wilson in *From Atlantis to the Sphinx*. If you would like to explore them further, please consult the books in Further Reading.) It is clear then that on the fringes of science there are to be found theories, ideas and evidence that support a magical approach. I feel I can state firmly that much of this nature is suppressed either by rejection or neglect, because it does not conveniently fit current paradigms.

USING MAGIC

Magic isn't the opiate of the ineffectual! If a person often reneges on promises (especially those they make to themselves about what they will do etc.), cheats on a partner, dodges, pilfers and lies, then they are unlikely to achieve much in circle. Starhawk explores this in *The Spiral Dance* (see Further Reading), making the point that if your word is to mean something in the subtle realms, then it has to mean something in the day-to-day. This isn't a matter of black-and-white morality, for on some occasions you may feel perfectly entitled to withhold the truth or to change your mind, but it is a matter of meaning what you say, doing what you intend, knowing what you are capable of, developing it and using it. It isn't about empty ego-inflation, but about human will and dignity, about moving among the gods. Because of this, magic has been feared and repressed. It can, and does, make people strong, independent and powerful. However, this power is 'power to' not 'power over'. This can be misinterpreted by people whose only concept of power is bossing others around! Such models belong to patriarchal structures, not to the domain of the witch, and witches have been feared possibly because their essence underlines what is unhealthy in such structures. However, magic has always been around and is there, unacknowledged, in simple prayers that most religions encourage. Going into a church or cathedral, lighting a candle and saying a prayer is a simple spell, 'spelling out' what you want and asking a higher power to grant it. The difference is in attitude, for the person who prays goes as a supplicant, while the witch is an activist. Being an activist isn't evil or disrespectful: it is using what you've got. Magic is the specific power point for the witch, and is the major sticking point for fundamentalist dogmas, and scientific dogmas, which can disempower us. The Goddess encourages Her children to grow up and go for it, for in doing so we draw closer to Her.

In magic it is fine to ask for things for yourself, because these are the gifts of the Goddess. Remember, all acts of love and pleasure are Her rituals. However, that doesn't mean that we work just for ourselves, or that we exalt our egos. A strange thing often happens when you do magic, and that is that the goal may become irrelevant, as you open out to greater reality. Experienced witches have been heard to say that they rarely bother with spells, because they feel in contact with the Goddess and that they are on their life path. In the end I believe the goal of all magic is union with the Goddess, our source, and is a mystical matter. Along the way, misfortune and failure will not dog you for working for your own comfort, unless you believe that it will. Having said this, spells should never be used to attempt to influence the will of another, and so in love spells, for instance, no attempt should be made to 'get' a specific person (especially if they already have a relationship with someone else), but the working should be general, about the kind of person you want, or the kind of life you wish to attract.

Does magic always work? Of course not. It takes much practice to work magic and much of that is about tuning into the unseen tides and realizing what it is suitable to work for and what it isn't. However, almost all magical working will achieve something, even if it isn't quite what we might wish. Here it is very important to be clear, for the unconscious mind is literal, and if you work for 'gold' you may get some nice gold wrapping paper, or a goldfish! Occult lore is full of stories of such quirky happenings. Another instance may be that what you ask for isn't quite what you hoped, such as in the case of a friend of mine who asked that her life might move on, because she felt stuck. It did, but not quite as she envisaged, for her secure relationship abruptly broke up, temporarily devastating her. However, looking back she can now see that it was what she needed in her life; she is really glad of it and has indeed 'moved on'. This is an example of how magic can work uncomfortably.

All acts of magic need a good deal of reflection and meditation, for in doing magic we take on a great responsibility, and good intentions may not be enough for protection from the consequences of thoughtless meddling. Exactly the same thing is true in everyday life. Some say it is best not to work magic for others, except in special circumstances, and even healing spells may have contra-indications, because we can never be sure where the illness or injury may be leading. Perhaps your friend needs to have flu, and a fortnight off work, and if she gets better too quickly, that could be the last straw to pitch her over into a breakdown, through stress! Of course this isn't to say 'don't' because some of the nicest spells may be healing spells, and we don't want to get frozen to the spot, debating negative possibilities. I think it is best to give things a little thought. Give your intuition opportunity to make itself heard. There aren't any absolute rules, but experience and pathworking will deepen your awareness. The mantic arts such as tarot and astrology can also help. Help and hints are all around, too! Recently I got into my car wondering about a certain course of action. Should I, shouldn't I? I turned on the ignition and pushed in my cassette, and Springsteen bellowed at me, 'It takes a leap of faith to get things going ... you gotta show some guts.' Well, well ...!

A final point that should be obvious, but isn't always, is that you must also take action in the outside world to back up your spell. Love spells by the dozen won't get you a lover if you don't go out, and spells to get a job aren't going to work if you don't apply for some.

THE SAFETY OF MAGIC

Orthodox religions often pontificate on the 'dangers' of the occult. Sadly, these dangers are often the self-fulfilling prophecies of religions that polarize 'light and dark' and teach about sin, hell and demons. I feel it is somewhat ironic that witches and pagans are suspected of corrupting the young, exposing them to immorality, drawing them into cults etc., when paganism is in reality very cult-free. The pagan mind dislikes the idea of the charismatic leader figure and the loss of individuality demanded by a cult. Further, modern pagans are almost paranoiac about involving young people, never initiating them before they reach 18 or 21 and offering very little in the form of guidance for teenagers whose energies are rampant and who are spiritually ravenous. On the other hand, fundamentalist groups tout for them while they're as young as possible. It was the Jesuits who said, 'Give me a child until he is five …' I have had a personal internal struggle, about whether I should remonstrate with my two elder sons about attending a young persons' evening organized by local fundamentalist Christians, whom I know are well-meaning people, but whom I also know are intent on getting conversions. Football, games and other entertainments are offered, to attract attendance, and it works! Afterwards, the young people have to sit through an obligatory session of Bible study. My boys wanted to go, and how could I possibly say 'no'? What was I afraid of?, I had to ask myself. I certainly didn't want them to 'get religion' and start berating me for my pentagrams etc., but I decided that I had to let them find their own path. They continue to go along, and continue to come home scoffing and giggling at the preaching part, which they regard as illogical and meaningless. I find myself remonstrating mildly with them about having respect for other people's faiths … However, on this subject, I feel the role of young people and witchcraft needs to be looked at seriously, for my mail shows me that many teenagers are drawn to the path, and they need guidance of some sort. Why should we withhold, while other religions forcefeed?

So, the main danger with magic concerns our own inner demons, which we absorbed along with the ABC, unless we were raised in a very enlightened manner. We are bound to have been contaminated with ideas about our own sinfulness, about something that will 'get' us if we don't toe the line, about law, retribution, being 'cast out', following Satan, or losing our souls. All of this is a great shame. However, if you try to tell yourself none of it applies to you, the chances are you will be doing yourself even more violence, forcing these images into your unconscious, and then you will surely meet them when you do magic, for magic will unleash them and psychism will reveal them. In *Circlework* (see Further Reading), Shan calls this the Magic Mirror, in which you see your own deepest fears, your most ineradicable programming. So, please be aware of this, go slowly, be gentle with yourself, accept your fears and work alongside and through them. Some hints for this are given at the end of Chapter 1.

Another danger with magic is that of ego-inflation, which can destroy a life and a personality. There are, it is true, a few people in the world of witchcraft and paganism who are on ego trips, to a greater or lesser extent, because witches and pagans are human, like everyone else. Pride in your growing magical awareness is fine and understandable; pride in your path and your liberty is, too. Trying to lord it over other people is just silly and will blind you to your own purpose. If you have wisdom, experience or valuable thoughts and feelings to impart, by all means do so. A teacher is one who offers, and who leads, not one who bosses. The real meaning of 'to educate' comes from the Latin *educere* meaning 'to draw out '. That's what we are doing when we teach, helping the other person to draw out what is already within them. This book is not about telling you things as much as helping you to find your own truth. Have proper pride in all things, by all means, but be humble and open also.

There are other safety issues regarding the raising of magical power that are common sense, such as grounding energy raised, and these are dealt with by following the steps for ritual, especially grounding and finishing off. Apart from this, I do feel that two important things are perspective and pathworking. Perspective is about keeping a balance, having a healthy mind in a healthy body, and so if you decide to take up the path of witchcraft, you are well advised to maintain sensible daily routines of eating, sleeping, working, cleaning, playing – not trying to become a full-time mystic overnight. Pathworking is about developing your inner sight. This comes slowly, with time, and will be your source of the greatest spiritual sustenance.

THE PATHWAY OF MAGIC

Jane Brideson, who illustrated this book, has developed the following 'magic map' as shown in the diagram opposite, and I cannot explain it in any better way. The matter starts (as far as we perceive) with our conscious Self, which we may also call the 'talking' 'middle' or 'waking' Self, which selects a goal that is in harmony with the True Will, and the purpose is conveyed to 'Younger Self' also known as the unconscious 'Lower Self' or subconscious through ritual and power-raising. Through the simple, unfettered medium of Younger Self the image and power are boosted and channelled to the Divine Self, which is our Higher Self, our eternal essence that partakes of the Goddess and the Cosmic Web. Our Divine Self uses the power to manifest or alter the exact purpose, through wisdom. The change is then experienced by the conscious Self, after a way has been opened in everyday life, such as creating opportunities, working, changing behaviour (e.g. applying for a job). And so another meaning of the 'magic circle' emerges, as this process completes itself in circular fashion, showing its manifestation in the place it originated, our everyday self. These ideas are developed to some extent from other writers listed in Further Reading, notably Shan and Starhawk.

Channels may be opened between the three selves in the following ways: Our conscious Self is concerned with speech, logic, intellect and the left side of the brain (in

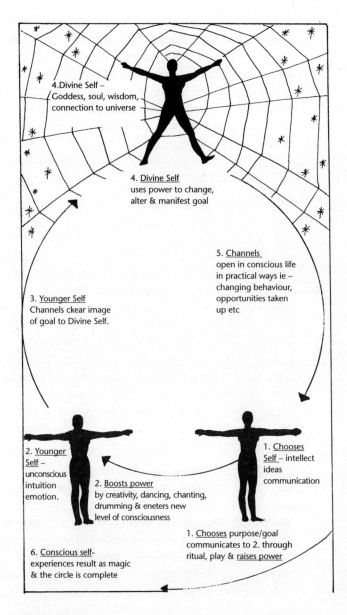

4.Divine Self – Goddess, soul, wisdom, connection to universe

4. <u>Divine Self</u>
uses power to change, alter & manifest goal

5. <u>Channels</u>
open in conscious life in practical ways ie – changing behaviour, opportunities taken up etc

3. <u>Younger Self</u>
Channels ckear image of goal to Divine Self.

2. <u>Younger Self</u> –
unconscious intuition emotion.

2. <u>Boosts power</u>
by creativity, dancing, chanting, drumming & eneters new level of consciousness

1. <u>Chooses Self</u> – intellect ideas communication

1. <u>Chooses</u> purpose/goal communicates to 2. through ritual, play & <u>raises power</u>

6. <u>Conscious self</u>-
experiences result as magic & the circle is complete

How magic works

right-handed people; this may be reversed for left-handed people). The right side of the brain connects to the left side of the body, and vice-versa, and the instinctual part of us thus connects to the more recessive side. By choosing to play, pathworking to meet our Younger Self or possibly animal representation such shamanic as power animals, and by looking at what gives pleasure, what we liked in childhood and perhaps dismantling some of the messages we received that inhibited our spontaneity, channels may be opened to Younger Self.

Younger Self is concerned with play, dreams, sex, creativity, music and pattern perception, and it connects with the right side of the brain and the left side of the body (in right-handed people). It can be helpful to ask yourself how you see this spontaneous, child-like, instinctual part of yourself. What sort of things were you told as a child? Do you have an internal image of yourself as 'bad', 'dirty', or similar, that your Everyday Self strives to 'polish up'? Rituals help Younger Self connect to Divine Self, and all activities where we put aside Everyday Self enable dialogue between these two parts of us, such as meditation, pathworking etc. Divine Self can then channel joy, freedom and enlightenment down through Younger Self. Counselling can also help break through some of Younger Self's grief and negative programming. Good relationships can also have a healing effect.

It is a good idea to ask ourselves how we imagine our Divine Self, in order to draw closer. Divine Self is the Goddess or God within and beyond, our connection with the infinite, our spiritual power source, a centre of calmness, joy and peace. Channels can open between Divine Self and Everyday Self by literally counting our blessings, working cognitively with our life-patterns (i.e. changing our ideas through a process of reason and common sense, realizing that we deserve good things, re-thinking what it may mean to be 'good' and also recognizing when it may be necessary to do without, not as a process of self-punishment but as a requisite for our life path).

This model has some connection with the parent/child/adult model of Transactional Analysis but it has spiritual connotations not necessarily involved in TA. Thinking of ourselves as this trinity and opening the channels between our different selves can be extremely creative, helping us to find balance and truth, and guiding us in our lives and our workings.

SPELLWORK

Witches usually refer to their rituals, circle-casting and spells as 'work' because it is! Magic needs a lot of effort and energy. However, magic should not leave you feeling drained at the end, but elated. When you start, however, it is not uncommon to feel drained, and if this happens maybe you need to review your methods of grounding, or attempt shorter, more focused workings. I find that magical working generally makes me feel great, all sparkly and sexy, but there are still times when sombre and heavy rituals can leave a 'hung over' feeling. This needs careful thought, and sometimes it is good to feel 'sombre'. Take things slowly, step by step, and always be prepared to review your methods.

Three things are important in spellwork: visualization, concentration and power. A fourth, perhaps, is confidence, for it is most important to remember that magic works in the direction of belief. This is explored in *Experimental Magic* by J.H. Brennan, listed in Further Reading. If you really do not believe that something can work, then there is no point in doing it, the only exception to this being that if your disbelief has relaxed you, it's amazing what does get through! Visualization is the ability clearly to envision the purpose of the spell as a reality. The simpler this is the better. If you can't visualize, use props and tell yourself with conviction and succinct description what is to be. You need to concentrate so you do not dissipate your energies or generate a fluffy image. Don't worry if you can't concentrate for long, because short bursts of intense concentration can be effective. Power really comes in two parts, which are, of course interconnected, but on different levels. One level is the mundane 'will power' which is a determination that this thing will be achieved, extending to the raising of magical power, which is really just lots of energy. Magic works through the power of the mind, clearly visualizing an outcome, concentrating upon it and focusing power upon that outcome.

A lot of magic works on the like-attracts-like principle, called Sympathetic Magic. When witches dance, raise a cone of power and send it off, there isn't much sign of sympathetic magic. However, for most spells, this is in evidence. Magic works by the practitioner saturating her or himself with the goal in mind, and this process is aided and amplified by harmonic props that help construct a vivid, mental image and also call in Younger Self, the instinctual part, in response. A simple example of this might be a spell for healing, where we rub a green candle with eucalyptus oil and light it, stating our intention to heal a friend. Eucalyptus is known as a healing oil, while green is a healing colour. To attract love we might wear a heart-shaped piece of rose quartz that we have consecrated earlier, burning candles of rose or soft blue surrounded by garlands of roses, using Venus-ruled substance such as thyme and ylang-ylang. If we are really serious about a ritual we can bring in as many other things as we can think of: erecting and decorating an entire altar to our purpose, wearing a robe and jewellery that corresponds, playing appropriate music, and displaying tarot and other cards that fit in. We can do all we can to fill ourselves and surround ourselves with the correct imagery and feelings until we are ready to send the spell off to do its work.

To help us in our spellwork there are tables of 'correspondences' to enable us to choose our trappings. These are usually grouped around planetary rulers, so it is helpful to select the most relevant planet for the working and go from there. You can link these also with the correspondences we looked at with the tools we use in magic (see Chapter 5). These are traditions, so treat them with respect, but not obedience, for your own instincts, in the end, will be your finest guide.

TABLE OF CORRESPONDENCES

Sun Health, protection, vitality, energy, legal matters, enlightenment, success, fulfilment, creativity, willpower. Orange or gold (some equate orange with Mercury but I do not). The astrological sign Leo. Lions, cats. Amber, carnelian, diamond, tiger's eye, sunstone. Bay, sunflower, cinnamon, benzoin, frankincense, juniper, copal. All deities connected with the Sun, e.g. Lugh, Grainne, Apollo. Sunday. Tarot Card – The Sun.

Moon Home, fertility, family, nurture, rhythm, instinct, natural reaction, healing, gardening, dreams, spirituality, love. White and silver (black could apply to waning/Dark Moon, red sometimes for Full Moon). The astrological sign Cancer. Fish, dolphins, snake, dog, bear. Aquamarine, chalcedony, quartz, moonstone, mother-of-pearl. Lemon, lemon balm, myrrh, eucalyptus, mallow. All deities connected to the Moon, although goddesses may differ according to phase and Moon-gods are hard to find, despite the fact that some say the Moon was originally masculine in many cultures. Diana, Artemis, Hecate, Selene, Thoth. Monday. Tarot Card – The High Priestess.

Mercury Intelligence, thought, reflection, communication, travel, study, eloquence, divination, wisdom, commerce. Yellow. The astrological signs Gemini and Virgo. Monkeys, swallows and all small, swift birds. Agate, aventurine, mottled jasper. Lavender, fennel, parsley, mace. Deities connected with travel and creative thought such as Mercury/Hermes, Bride. Wednesday. Tarot Card – The Magician.

Venus Love, harmony, beauty, youth, joy, happiness, reconciliation, pleasure, friendship, compassion, meditation. Blue, pink/rose, also green. The astrological signs Taurus and Libra. Doves, swans. Emerald, lapis lazuli, turquoise. Thyme, rose, ylang-ylang, magnolia, feverfew, and many fragrant five-petaled blooms. Gods and goddesses of love and beauty, Aphrodite, Oshun, Adonis, Freya, Edain. Friday. Tarot Card – The Empress.

Mars Courage, energy, assertion, healing (after surgery), desire, passion, sexuality, strength, defense, exorcism. Red. The astrological signs Aries and Scorpio. Rams, scorpions, horses. Bloodstone, flint, red jasper, garnet, ruby. Wormwood, ginger, basil, peppermint, cumin. Gods and goddesses of war, Thor, Ares, Valkyries, Amazons, Moorigan. Thursday. Tarot Card – The Tower.

Jupiter Prosperity, good fortune, luck, justice, legal settlements, spiritual and religious matters, philosophy, long-distance travel, psychism, meditation, expansion, positive attitude. Purple. The astrological signs Sagittarius and Pisces. Centaur, horse, eagle. Amethyst, lepidolite. Sage, clove. Goddesses and gods of majesty, justice and luck, Juno, Zeus, Ishtar, Felicitas, Kuan-Yin (note that Kuan-Yin has many meanings and is one of the more 'complete' goddess-forms). Tuesday. Tarot Card – Wheel of Fortune.

Saturn Binding, grounding, protecting, centering, purifying, nurturing, fertilizing, actualizing, ending, preserving, certain kinds of luck, solidity, restriction. Black, grey, dark brown, dark green and possibly dark blue. The astrological signs Capricorn and Aquarius. Goats and horned animals. Apache tear, jet, onyx, obsidian. Comfrey, patchouli, cypress. Goddesses and gods of necessity, fate, cosmic order but also harvest, Cernunnos, Maat, Nokomis. Saturday. Tarot Card – The World.

The extra-Saturnian planets Uranus, Neptune and Pluto are still being worked with to ascertain where they correspond and if you are well up on their meanings you could incorporate these, although I can't recommend specifics. Uranus has links with Mercury and Sun, Neptune with Venus and Moon, and Pluto with Mars, but this is very general indeed. However, it could help with choice of incense etc. In respect of deities, as you find out more about the attributes of your favourites, you may like to incorporate them in your own ways. Note also, associations overlap and mingle somewhat.

A SIMPLE EXAMPLE

An example of a spell to give you greater energy after you've had a period, 'the blues' or an illness might include gold or orange candles, incense of frankincense, cinnamon and jupiter with a pinch of eucalyptus, lots of gold and orange props such as a picture of the sun (or the Tarot Card), sunflowers (but not van Gogh's melancholy rendering), gold/orange altar cloth and anything else you can think of. After casting your circle in the usual way, you may like to raise energy and direct it into an amber stone, which you then wear around your neck. You might also just like to sit, feeling the warmth and brightness enter your being, chanting, 'Get up and go, get into me' or something similar. This could be one spell you might choose to perform in sunlight.

Although simple, this is a good example of the care needed in spellwork, and how the goal needs to be carefully thought out and formulated. For instance, a spell with lots of bright imagery could be too much and counter-productive if we still have some healing and recovering to complete, and we might feel more depleted by its demands. In this case a healing approach at Full Moon or during a waxing Moon, using green or white candles, incorporating more healing substances such as lemon balm in the incense, might be better. Spells are more fully discussed in *Spells and Rituals:*

A Beginner's Guide and incense in *Herbs for Magic and Ritual* *A Beginner's Guide* which are listed in Further Reading.

RAISING THE POWER

The power used in magic is very hard to define and I do not feel that we have the words or the developed consciousness to encompass fully what happens. It is actually something that often comes instinctively, especially when we are children. To me, the idea of 'raising power' has always been bit of a block, rather as if someone, when telling you to 'Step over here' prefaces it by saying, 'Send an electrical impulse from your brain to your leg, and then stand over here!' When I was a child I used to do little spells by concentrating on something I wanted, over and over again in my mind until something was released in a kind of burst and I knew could do no more, and that I would get what I wanted. I called it 'my prayer being heard' and I do not remember it ever not working. Recently, discussing this with a friend, she pointed out that what I was instinctively doing, as a child, was raising power by chanting, albeit silently and internally.

One of the strongest sensations of 'power' that I have encountered came not in circle (where one might expect it and therefore not be taken aback) but at a school disco that I helped with, when my eldest son was in his last year at junior school. The hall was packed with pre-adolescents, crackling with excitement, and the atmosphere was breathtaking. When the music started there was a huge burst of energy that nearly blew me away. Some parents looked frazzled, but some of us loved it! In the very 'old days' events like this would have been held outdoors, perhaps under a Full Moon, and directed towards a communal cause, such as a good crop yield. Perhaps one of the reasons we sometimes feel spent and dissipated is because we do not direct such energy, but leave it spilling out all over the place, ungrounded. In circle all such energy is contained and concentrated. The energy has been called 'prana', 'orgone', 'chi', 'life force' – we are all familiar with *Star Wars* and 'The force be with you'! These are all more or less the same energy, it seems to me. It is within all of us. Even if you do not specifically raise energy in circle, there will have been energy put into casting the circle, and this needs to be consciously grounded, returned to the earth as a healing force.

The best way to understand magic is to see it as something that draws its power from the etheric energy of the individual, Earth and cosmos, drawn up and magnified through the chakras (which we shall explore below), and focused by the imagination. There are various ways of raising power in this way. Dancing and chanting are two of them, and if done communally, a bonding of the group mind takes place at an unconscious level. Rhythmic gesture can also work, such as stirring motions, and this may be used by lone practitioners. Much power is also raised during sex, and, of course, released at death, hence the horrible rites sometimes reported by the newspapers, involving the sacrifice of some poor animal in a churchyard. These rites are not usually, it would seem, undertaken by people who know what they are doing, but who rather enjoy being shocking. They certainly are not witchcraft rites, for witches love and respect animals and affirm life.

The magical power raised exists in the ether, and may be seen by clairvoyants as violet light or golden light. Its presence may be sensed, and part of the art of spellworking can be to recognize the moment at which to release the power. The power is directed by the imagination towards the purpose of the working. For instance, for a working concerned with world peace, you might choose to place some white rose petals in your cauldron, at the centre of your circle, dance around this and direct the energy into the petals, with your hands (you could use your athame if you wish, but may like to use both hands). Later you could scatter the petals outdoors, affirming that they are a peaceful influence upon the Earth. Alternatively, you might visualize your power rising in a cone, and shooting off, at the appropriate moment, to help a specific area. A more sedentary example could be some cord magic, where you tie knots in a cord, and in so doing you are raising power by your actions, although you may also wish to top it up in some way, perhaps again by dancing or chanting.

Imagination is important for spells. Imagination is not, of course, flimsy wishful thinking but an important creative act, for everything that is worthwhile, enjoyable and beautiful in our lives existed first in our imagination. A distinction could perhaps be made here between the sort of 'imagination' that daydreams that we have won the lottery (although that, too can become purposeful), and the imaginative faculty that produces works of art and impressions of Otherworld and its creatures. Imagination is our gateway to the astral planes, and in these realms magical effects first take shape, extending gradually into everyday life.

I am sure you will discover more about the power raised and the way you perceive it and deal with it as you practise. If you start with small rituals and always remember to ground yourself, you will be fine. If you have no 'sense' of the power, that is because your conscious mind is filtering it out, and the best way to deal with this is the 'as if' approach. Behave 'as if' you were able to sense the power, direct it and ground yourself. Eventually your sense will grow, or more likely you will realize that it was there all along! Please don't expect sudden flashes or blinding visions, for this awareness more likely to grow gradually.

Power can be raised in any way that raises energy, by dancing, chanting, clapping, humming. Traditionally witches dance in a circle, holding hands and chanting. The energy can be sensed, rising in a golden cone that becomes white gold and shoots off to do its work. In a coven the High Priestess will direct when the energy has risen to its height and needs to be released. I have to say that descriptions of this power seem to vary enormously and doubtless depend on the perceptions of each individual. Some do describe the power as a rainbow, or as a blue-purple light, and some descriptions are quite complex. I can only say that my perception is of a golden light.

Power-raising can be summarized as follows:

- The power is your life force, and the life force around and within the Earth.

- It is generated by your intent and your actions.

- It is directed by your will and imagination.

- It is perceived as a force-field, coloured light (usually gold or violet), flames or sparks. Unless you are clairvoyant you probably won't 'see' it literally. The power can also be sensed, in the same way we sense atmospheres when we go into a room where people have been arguing, or making love.

- This power is quite natural and it is an intensification of something that is there all the time. Take your time to get acquainted with it.

THE ROLE OF THE CHAKRAS

The chakras are organs in the spiritual/astral body, or energy centres. The word *chakra* means 'wheel' or 'spin'. In a sense we might understand the chakras as interface points with the physical realms and the subtle planes. We can locate them in the physical body, but they would not be visible to a surgeon. There is more than one chakra system in existence, for instance, some specify eight or ten chakras, while some place a chakra below the feet, and other variations. In addition, besides the main chakras there are many other smaller energy centres around the body. Here we shall be working with seven chakras, because I and others have found this to work.

Learning to open your chakras may take a long time or it may happen almost immediately. Opening the chakras intensifies your awareness of the subtle planes and gives you greater access to the energies that are all round, and come from within the great body of Earth herself. Awakening these centres is part of a process of spiritual enlightenment along your path as a witch. The chakras are explored in *Chakras for Beginners* by Naomi Ozaniec (see Further Reading), and it is certainly a good idea to explore the meanings of the chakras in more detail than room permits here.

The base chakra is situated at the bottom of the spine and the colour associated with it is red. It rules the basic instincts and the 'fight or flight' adrenal glands. The second chakra is located in the lower abdomen and linked to sex, reproduction and intimacy (although I feel that sex is also related to the base chakra in some respects). The second chakra is orange. The third chakra is gold/yellow and coincides with the solar plexus, behind the navel, ruling the life-force, willpower and 'centering'. The fourth heart chakra is concerned with love and compassion and is situated in the chest, and is green in colour. The fifth chakra, at the base of the throat, is blue and connects with communication and creativity. In the centre of the forehead is the sixth chakra, coloured indigo and associated with intuition, while the seventh violet-coloured chakra, also called the 'many-petaled lotus', is found just above the head and is linked to enlightenment and mysticism.

Eastern teachings seem to speak of the chakras in a way that is rather different from witchcraft, almost as if the opening of the chakras is something for the spiritually adept. Of course you do need to be spiritually aware and open to activate your chakras, but it is well within the reach of the ordinary person who wishes to progress. Witches activate their chakras for trancework, magic and healing. The 'Earth force', or however you wish to describe it, may be drawn up through the base chakra, and this can give a feeling of oceanic calm coupled with immense vitality.

Opening the chakras may take a while, and so it is best to start with daily practice, concentrating first on the base chakra. Chakra-opening can be obtained with relaxation practice which we shall cover in the following chapter. It is best to practise this for five minutes every day, rather than a marathon stretch every Sunday. You need to be able to relax completely. Ensure that you will not be disturbed, because it can be very disorientating to be suddenly interrupted when your chakras are open, and you could get a bad head and feel very irritable. Concentrate upon visualizing the chakra at the base of the spine, feel its colour flood through you, feel it pulse, glow and grow. Keep relaxing, visualizing and feeling peaceful, even if you don't think anything is happening. The opening of the chakra may not be dramatic. It may start as a feeling of excitement, of opening out, growing and belonging – a blossoming that becomes huger and huger. Don't worry if nothing seems to happen for it may need several attempts.

If you feel your first chakra open, the red colour may seem to flood you and there may be an immense feeling of openness and wonderment. This may even bring tears to your eyes (although that happens more readily with the heart chakra). Stay with the base chakra for a while, and only move on to the next chakra when you feel sure the chakra is fully open and you have experienced it. The sensation is pleasurable. Usually, after the first chakra opens, the rest follow reasonably easily. Take your time with this, relaxing and enjoying.

When all the chakras are open then energy from the Earth, or the cosmos that surrounds us, may be drawn up through them. As you set this in motion you may physically twitch, as if with a mild electric shock. There will be a power surge that runs through you. Picture the power as a fountain of light issuing in a shower from the crown and returning into the solar plexus chakra, so that the power circulates as in a battery. You will feel as if you are electrified. This energy can be used to enhance your spellwork; you may use it in healing (for instance, if you touch a bruise on a friend or loved one the chances are that it will heal much quicker, or cold may ease or a headache may lift), or you can open your chakras before doing pathworking.

When you are used to opening your chakras, you will be able to open them quickly, in preparation for a ritual. The chakras must always be carefully closed because if they are not you could feel sick, drained or get a migraine if you come into contact with disruptive energies. Chakras can be closed by eating and drinking, and all the other grounding exercises such as patting yourself all over, touching the ground etc. all help. Visualize your chakras closing like eyes, or flower petals in the rain, or whatever imagery appeals. Close them one by one, starting at the crown and working down. Affirm shutdown, close off, switch off. The chakras are an important area of development and study, and while some books on witchcraft do not mention them, I feel they are often opened instinctively by witches.

STEP BY STEP

Here is a step by step checklist to follow for rituals and magical work:

1 Clearly identify your goal. This may need several days to reflect if it is an important ritual. Remember, the unconscious is very literal. If you concentrate on a new house, for instance, a friend could give you a nice new pottery cottage as a present. What you probably want

is a better home. Allow at least one night to dream about the matter, and even if you do not remember dreaming you will probably wake up feeling clearer. Keep a notepad by the bed for first thoughts. You may wish also to do a pathworking.

2   Plan your ritual. Write down what you will need. Think about correspondences. If you aren't good at this, stay with basics.

3   Choose a time when you won't be interrupted. Check the Moon phase (and other planetary conditions, if you know some astrology). For most rituals night time is best.

4   Assemble your tools. These will be all your usual requirements for circle-casting, plus the extras for this ritual. It is best to write your list down. Include matches.

5   Prepare yourself. A cleansing bath with salt or lavender added is excellent. Put on ritual garments. Meditate for a little. Open your chakras.

6   Create and cleanse your circle.

7   Invoke the Elemental Powers.

8   Ask for the blessing of your own goddesses or gods.

9   Now you are proceeding with you particular spell or ritual. Clearly state your intention. Imagine, concentrate, will, but also relax, for any tension will block you. Remember there is a playful element in everything. Raise power in whatever way you have chosen, or the working entails. Direct and release the spell.

10 Let go. Let it wing on its way. This needs to be done consciously, or the energy raised may hang around.

11 Commune with the Goddess and give thanks.

12 Give thanks and say farewell to the Guardians/elements/ Watchtowers. You may do more than one ritual at once (personally I like to do several), having gone to the trouble of constructing the circle. It is good to do one for yourself, one for a friend and one for the world or community (work for a friend may just mean sending love, which is pretty safe!). Three is probably the most

it is advisable to attempt at once, but again you can go with how you feel. When all is complete, and you have communed, dismantle your circle.

13 Make a special exercise of grounding yourself by placing your palms on the ground and imagining all the extra energy running out into the earth like water. Pat yourself all over, starting with the top of your head. Eat and drink something. Affirm that you are back in the everyday world.

TRAINING SESSION 8

Chants As we have seen, a favourite means of raising power is by chanting. You can make up your own chant, if you prefer, or you could just simply repeat something very basic like 'Power up, power up, power up …'. Rhymes need to scan well, run smoothly. Here is one of my own, given in *Witchcraft: A Beginner's Guide*.

> *Pentacle and Earth and North*
> *Call the cone of magic forth*
> *Air and East athame bright*
> *Cone of magic to its height*
> *Fire and South and candle burn*
> *Make the cone of magic turn*
> *Cauldron deep and west and water*
> *Cone of magic never falter*
> *Aya aya Anu, aya aya Lugh*
> *Aya aya Anu, aya aya Lugh*

The last pair of lines can be repeated until you feel the power has reached the right point, and the names are chosen mainly for their sound. Anu is one of the Celtic Great Mother goddesses and Lugh (pronounced Loo) is a Celtic god of light and craft.

My favourite chant is well known to witches and is used routinely in Wiccan covens. It is by Doreen Valiente and called *The Witches' Rune*.

Darksome night and shining Moon
East then South then West then North
Harken to the witches' rune
Here I come to call thee forth

Earth and Water, Air and Fire
Wand and pentacle and sword
Work ye unto my desire
Harken ye unto my word

Cords and censer, scourge and knife
Powers of the witches' blade
Waken all ye unto life
Come ye as the Charge is made

Queen of Heaven, Queen of Hell
Horned Hunter of the night
Lend your power unto my spell
Work my will by magic rite

By all the powers of land and sea
By all the might of Moon and Sun
As I do will, so mote it be
Chant the spell and be it done

Eko, eko, Azarak
Eko, eko, Zamilak
Eko, eko, Karnayna
Eko, eko, Aradia.

Although Azarak and Zamilak are meaningless (as far as I know, Karnayna is a name for the Horned God and Aradia for the Goddess. A chant can be meaningless, like kids in a playground, or words can be used as an evocation, visualizing 'powers of land and sea', which add voltage to our efforts. Some call this a 'making'.

Another suggestion is made by the priestess Shan in *Circlework* (see Further Reading).

This is to sing the following to the tune of 'Three Blind Mice':

> *Goddess and God*
> *Goddess and God*
> *I am their child*
> *I am their child*
> *Goddess and God*
> *Goddess and God.*

Your chants do not have to sound musical: they are a way of raising energy and celebrating the Goddess. You can be sure she is smiling, just like any mother smiles when her child sings even if her little one has a voice like a drain! You can have fun with your chants. Use this training session to learn and practise one of your choice, or compose one yourself.

Chakra work   It is a good idea to begin chakra work. Look ahead to the instructions for relaxation, given in the next chapter, and use these as a prelude to opening your chakras.

Spellwork   Practise composing some simple spells of your own.

CURSES

This seems like a good point on which to recap on ethics. Please don't ever contemplate cursing another person. It is a gross misuse of your subtle skills and will probably result in you losing them. The path of the witch is about individuality and freedom, and that is infringed if we seek to influence the destiny of another. Usually curses don't work, because they need the co-operation, at least at an unconscious level, of the cursed person. Because of this, in most magical systems, the person who is cursed is unmistakably informed about what is going on, and then all that is needed is for their beliefs to do their work, bringing them into decline. Some people assert that a curse can only work if the accursed knows about it, but I doubt this, and there are some documented cases of people who were apparently able to curse, almost without meaning to and without any awareness on the part of the receiver. The abilities of John Cowper Powys are a case in point, and he developed an attitude of 'neurotic benevolence' because of the misfortunes that seemed to befall those he had a grudge against! However, such cases are a rarity, and mostly it is very hard to curse effectively, because each individual has an etheric 'skin' that protects them, and an unconscious that operates a bit like a kick-boxing guardian angel, to repel all attack! This is strongest when we are well-balanced and healthy. Occult law states that what we do comes back to us, off the heel of this kick boxer. Actually, the nasty vibes of curses and the visualization necessary for them ensure that those who attempt to curse are acting to their own detriment from 'circle one'. There is never any need for cursing. Live well is the best revenge. Spells should be positive, to take you forward. On rare occasions where someone needs to be dealt with, such as a murderer or rapist, there may be occasion for binding spells, undertaken by a group, or a spell to bring the person to justice. But spells themselves are not about dispensing retribution, but about obtaining what is legitimate for us, among other things.

9

PATHWORKING
AND SCRYING

> *Your hearts know in silence the secrets of the days*
> *and the nights.*
> *But your ears thirst for the sound of your*
> *heart's knowledge.*
> *You would know in words that which you have*
> *always known in thought.*
> *You would touch with your fingers the naked*
> *body of your dreams.*

KAHLIL GIBRAN, *THE PROPHET* (1923)

PATHWORKING

In Chapter 3 we first encountered the idea of pathworking. Pathworking is the activity of making an inner journey. This inner journey is also a journey to the most far-flung and wildest places, to the most peaceful places and to the most hidden, mysterious and revealing, for we go 'inside' ourselves in order to go fully more outside, in our 'dreambody' into the realms of spirit and Otherworld.

Pathworking is arguably the most important activity of the witch because it is in this way that we find our truth and our direction. Pathworking can take us to meet our own special goddesses and gods, and connect us to wider reality. The inner journeys we make can have many different uses. We may pathwork to experience a feeling of peace, to connect more deeply with the natural world, to explore our inner powers, to get a better idea of our life path, to seek wisdom and enlightenment, to meet deities, to obtain answers and, in the case of group work, to achieve greater bonding between group members. Another example of what we could term a pathwork could be an inner journey to meet an animal or plant deva. A deva is a term meaning a powerful Nature spirit that has dominion over a species, at least in a specific locality. An example of this arose in the Findhorn Community in Scotland, where highly successful attempts were made to co-operate with Nature and to work on an energy level. The community were troubled by moles so a 'journey' was made to an awesome being called 'King Mole' and an undertaking given that the moles would be left alone if they left the garden alone. This worked, and the moles moved off to the surrounding scrubland. I have found such journeys to be successful too in discouraging insects (although these can be scary encounters), and friends have repeatedly got rid of ants by the same method.

Such journeys are perhaps better called shamanic journeys, whereas pathworking is usually more about developing one's inner sight and abilities, and sense of connection with the eternal and spiritual. Some pathworking is highly structured, whereas some merely contains some triggering suggestions. Pathworking on the Qabalah can also be performed, where each of the paths of the Tree of Life is covered. The Qabalah is an ancient Hebrew mystical tradition upon which some witches draw, and the Tree of Life is its basis. The Tree of Life is, in a way, a diagram of manifestation from purest spirit down to physical form, and it is made up of ten Sephiroth (singular Sephira), or spheres, connected by 22 paths, each of which are linked to a card from the Major Arcana of the tarot. Each Sephira represents a specific energy or stage and is linked to one of the planets. This can be thought of as a map of Creation – a blueprint of the process of bringing into being any activity or situation – or also a kind of plan of the inner make-up of the individual.

The Tree of Life is shown in the diagram, along with the planetary correspondence of each Sephira. 'Correspondence'

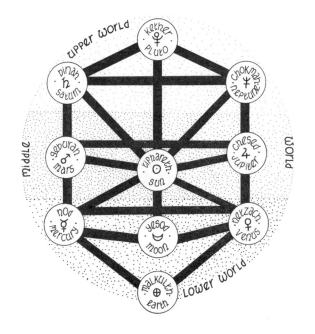

The Tree of Life

is a significant word, for much in our system of correspondences derives from Qabalistic thought. As the Tree of Life is also a diagram of the psyche the paths can be travelled in a system of pathworking. Such exploration can be very revealing and far-reaching. However, by no means all witches have an interest in the Qabalah. Some feel it is rather a formal system, and prefer simpler methods. It is the simpler approach which we shall explore.

RELAXATION

One of the most important magical exercises is that of learning to unwind. Perhaps the greatest barrier to the development of occult skills is the tension produced by everyday life, and if we wish to become more open we need to learn true relaxation. It is well known that moments of greatest inspiration come, not when our foreheads are screwed up in concentration, but when we let go, look at the sunset, listen to music and let ourselves meld with the fullness of life. Conscious relaxation is a valuable skill to learn.

To acquire this skill, please commit yourself to daily practice. Here you are trying to get a message through to your unconscious, your Younger Self, and like all children, Younger Self learns by repetition. Five minutes a day is much better than an hour once a week, which is unlikely to achieve much at all except a pleasant doze. Choose a realistic, convenient time of day, when you won't be disturbed. Your bed is probably the best place to start as it tells your mind to 'sleep'. However, as you become more adept, move to a chair, for the purpose here is conscious relaxation, not unconscious! If you let up on your routine, forgive yourself and start again. Yes, discipline is important, but this isn't an all-or-nothing regimen. You wouldn't give up cleaning your teeth because you forgot one night. Regular effort will yield the best and the quickest results.

Once stretched out, relaxation ought to be easily achieved, but it isn't. Most of us are a mass of unacknowledged tension and we all have our favourite trouble spots, like the shoulders, jaw (or in the case of 'anal retentives' the buttocks!) You may be aware of yours. If so, proceed to this spot with love and let the tension dissolve. There are various ways of going through your body and some people advocate that you tense each muscle to an unbearable pitch and then relax. Fine if this works, but I feel more tense as a result. You may simply go through each area of your body, starting at the toes and working slowly upwards. You may visualize that your muscles are powered by tiny men who are downing tools and walking off. You may use imagery, such as floating on a stream… the water flows beneath you… now you sink sweetly beneath it… it flows through you… you become one with the water… you are the water, flowing downstream… You may feel yourself suspended on the cosmic web, gently and totally partaking of the 'everythingness'. You may use a combination of methods. One good idea is to record instructions on a tape or get a soft-spoken friend to do this, if you don't like your voice. When your method is complete, review your body again to make sure no tension has crept back. Pay special attention to your face, scalp and neck for there are many muscles here and it is easy for tension to find its way back.

BREATHING

When you feel reasonably sure that you are properly relaxed (if you have not done this before, several weeks of daily practice are recommended), you can start some simple breathing exercises. No strain should be experienced at any time and if this arises, stop. One of the most important things to remember is to breathe out fully, because all too often we hold a bit of our breath, especially when we are tense (asthma is said to be the inability to breathe out, rather than in). It is as if we want to hold onto what breath we have in case we can't get another! Breathing out fully is an exercise of trust in the Universe. Simply breathe in to a count of four, hold in to a count of two, breathe out to a count of four and hold out to the count of two. Regulate the speed of your counting so that it suits you and hold your breath by the abdominal muscles, not by closing your throat. Don't overdo this at first and if you feel 'funny' at any time, give it a rest.

Even this small exercise will have begun to alter your body chemistry beneficially. After 50–70 sessions of this breathing linked-to-relaxation, an automatic association will have taken root in the unconscious, so that when you go to rhythmic breathing you instinctively relax. This is a great prelude to magical work, or pathworking. It is also very handy in life, when you need to calm down, and can be a practical occultist's 'trick'.

YOUR SANCTUARY

Having learnt to relax, and to deepen that relaxation with your breathing, perhaps the most useful and creative bit of pathworking on which to embark is that of building your sanctuary. In a sense, this is not regular pathworking, which is more receptive, but more purposeful. However, it will stand you in good stead, being an important exercise in visualization and a solid bastion on the astral plane. Do not tell anyone else what your sanctuary is like, unless you trust them completely, and personally even then I would not speak of it.

If you have become used to deep relaxation you will probably have found that images arise in you spontaneously, like a waking dream, and you may have found these useful. In fact, you may already be used to travelling the inner planes. If not, please refer back to the Training Session at the end of Chapter 3, and let the curtain rise on the natural world. However, this time you are not merely an observer. You are going to enter this world. Look all about you. Breathe deeply of the air, notice the sights and the sounds and feel the sun on your skin. You may like to spend time doing this, and to record instructions on a tape.

You are going to go to a place. It is the safest, most beautiful place you have ever been. This will not necessarily be some glamourous holiday destination, but somewhere that really feels right. You may review several scenes before deciding, rather like flicking through an astral travel brochure. When an image arises that really feels good, go there completely, leaving behind your first entry point.

Is your sanctuary there before you, or is this the place where you know you must build it? If the former, take note of all the characteristics of the sanctuary, in detail. Look, affirm, describe, wonder. This is your very own place, and will always be safe. Visualize it becoming stronger and stronger, as you look. Surround it with golden light, pentagrams or whatever you wish. When you are ready, go inside and explore or construct. Take as much time as you need to make this as solid as possible. Don't worry if at first things shift, melt and change quite a bit. This is a place of safety and beauty and each time you go there it is becoming stronger.

If your sanctuary needs to be built, do so, and when you have completed it, follow the steps above. If frightening, destructive, confusing or doubtful feelings or images arise, accept them, form a pentagram in the air and place a protective circle about yourself so they cannot get too close. It is a good idea to do exercises such as this within a ritual circle that you have previously constructed. If you have problems, ask for help of the Goddess, or your own special inner guide, to help you. If you have difficulties, try to learn what these may mean about you, and keep a note in your Book of Shadows.

Spend the time needed to construct your astral sanctuary with reasonable detail and do this perhaps half a dozen times, before moving on to other pathworking when you feel ready. It is good to have within your sanctuary a special robe that you put on for your travels. Always remember, when you finish any pathworking, to give yourself time to come back to the everyday world. Do the eating and drinking, patting and placing palms to the floor that you do to ground yourself after rituals. If you have opened your chakras, close these thoroughly.

An alternative to the sanctuary I have described could be a place you know very well, or can imagine very well, in the natural world, and one that you love deeply. Shamanic teachings state that this needs to have an entry to Upperworld, which could be a tree, a rainbow or anything on which you might 'travel upwards', and an entry to a Lower World, such as a cave or burrow. Although this place exists, did exist or might well exist in the everyday world, it is, in fact, situated in Middle World. Make sure that you can visualize this place in as much detail and as vividly as possible and that it is a secure and safe spot for you. You may go here to commence all your journeys and pathworking. If you choose to meet and to journey with power animals, this is the place to start from, and your animal will come to you, as you wait. Sometimes it can be very interesting to wait and see which animal arrives, because this can tell us a lot about what we need at present. If you wish to pathwork in a very unstructured way, you can simply go to this place with a definite purpose in mind. You might ask, 'I want more clarity in my current relationship, or, 'Should I do a ritual to find out the way forward?' and go where you feel led. You may receive an answer that is very clear, you may be shown a set of symbols, meet certain creatures, go to important places – or very little may happen and all may appear confused. If so, you may journey again and again to ask for answers, or to ask what symbols meant. Many people like to journey to the beat of a drum, but that isn't obligatory. This subject is covered more fully in *Shamanism: A Beginner's Guide* (see Further Reading).

THE HALLS OF WISDOM

You may like to record the following text to help in your relaxation on a tape.

Relax, centre down, breathe in rhythm if you wish and open your chakras. Enter your sanctuary or go to your special place. (Please note, whether your sanctuary is a boat in the middle of the ocean, an underground grotto or an aeroplane in flight, there can and will be ways to ascend from it, so take the time to clarify this.)

You are going on an important journey. Put on your robe. From your sanctuary you go out and upwards, so that your feet are wending their way steadily up a mountain path. Take the time to look around you, smell the mountain air, see the fresh plant-life that grows this high up and note the rocks that lie rough beneath your feet, the blueness of the sky and the free sound of the wind. [Pause.]

Continuing onwards and upwards you see something glinting on the path ahead. Slowly you approach it and you find that it is a silver ankh, shaped at the base like a key. Place this in the pocket of your robe and continue. [Pause.]

Now the air is becoming cooler. The path you have traversed is shrouded in mist behind you, and also before you. The ground is becoming more rugged and bare. On and on you climb. Notice anything that is around you at present. [Pause.]

As you climb even higher, the air seems to be acquiring a golden glow. Far away you can hear a soft, melodic tinkling, like windchimes. Coming around a rocky outcrop you find yourself confronted by a wooden door, large, brown and solid, shaped like an arch at the top. You push it but it does not give. You notice a keyhole and finger the ankh key in your pocket. Do you wish to use the key?

If the answer is 'Yes' place the key in the lock and feel it turn, smoothly. The great door swings open revealing a temple precinct. Replace the key in your pocket as the door swings shut behind you. Here a clear stream runs between emerald lawns. The windchimes you heard are to be seen, hanging from willow trees. Ahead of you there is a path, not rough and arduous like the one you have just climbed, but smooth as marble. The path leads to a bridge that crosses the

*stream. It leads in turn to some steps that mount to a
great, low platform. Over the platform is a conical roof.
At the front, the roof is supported by columns, but
around the sides it is surrounded by circular walls,
covered with carvings. From this structure a low
chanting emanates. There is a scent of incense. Apart
from this, all is stillness. There is an atmosphere of
peace and gentleness. [Pause.]*

*When you feel ready, follow the path over the bridge to
the steps and climb them. Now you can see into the
temple, although the light is dim. The chanting gains
in strength and you feel it resonate in your bones.
Candles flicker in the recesses, and you see a semi-
circle of thrones, 13 in number, on which shadowy
figures sit, motionless. [Pause.]*

*From the shadows behind the thrones a figure emerges
and approaches you slowly. Although you know this is
a creature of love, you feel a sense of awe. The being
draws close to you. Take note of her or him, with
respect. This being will have a gift for you, or will have
something important to say. Take very careful note,
and give thanks. [Pause.]*

*Saying a respectful farewell, leave the temple, going
slowly back along the path, over the bridge and out
through the door. Close it softly behind you. Go down
the mountain path. Replace the ankh key on the path,
where you found it, and return to your sanctuary.*

Take off your robe and return to everyday awareness. Make
a note of your gift/message in your Book of Shadows.

TO MEET THE ELEMENTS

To achieve a deeper understanding of the four elements,
you may like to do this pathworking.

Enter your sanctuary, put on your robe and prepare for a journey. [Pause.]

Come out of your sanctuary and find yourself on a meadow path, heading towards woodland. The air is heavy with the scent of elderflower and alive with the scuttling of small creatures in the undergrowth. Underfoot the grass is thick and rustly. Many wildflowers grow, daisies, clover, dandelions. This is a lush and fertile place. [Pause.]

As you approach the woodland, the grass thins out under the shadows of the trees. You approach a stone wall, clamber over and find yourself in the wood. The smell of the soil is rich and thick. The air is still. All around you there is an expectant quiet. [Pause.]

You continue into the wood, and the branches of the trees form a tangled roof over your head, blocking out the Sun. The ground becomes more rough, rocky and uneven, with stony outcrops and the twisted roots of the trees rising like petrified serpents from the ground. [Pause.]

Ahead of you the ground rises and you are aware of a patch of darkness which takes shape as the mouth of a cave. You approach this cave with awe. The breath of the earth exhales to meet you. All is darkness as you feel your way along the cold and rugged walls of the cave, going deep within the Earth. [Pause.]

Gradually the tunnel opens out so that you cannot reach both sides at once. Touching the left wall, you continue. Very slowly the light grows, as if the walls themselves are luminous. Rounding a corner, you suddenly find yourself in a vast, underground chamber. The ceiling disappears up into a darkness pierced only by the sharp points of enormous stalactities, while stalagmites grow upwards to meet them. You are in a secret, underground temple, formed by Nature. [Pause.]

At the far end of the chamber you notice that there is a great pile of precious stones, glowing and twinkling with all the colours of the rainbow, lit by inner fires. Rubies, garnets, carnelian, amber, agate, emeralds, lapis lazuli, amthysts, rose quartz, diamonds and many, many others vie with each other in beauty and vibrancy. You approach these stones, as if magnetized.

Now you become aware that you are not alone in the chamber. Beings emerge, which dwell there, the powers of Elemental Earth, Gnomes and Nature spirits. Greet them with great respect and spend as much time there as you and they feel comfortable with, conversing or otherwise communicating, or just watching. These beings may have a message or a gift for you. If so, receive it with joy and thanks and pledge a gift in return, such as planting a tree, tending an overgrown spot or anything that seems appropriate. Leave with thanks and respect, only when it feels right. Choose whether you wish to return to your sanctuary and everyday awareness or whether you wish to continue.

If you wish to continue, notice another opening, beyond the pile of jewels, and walk towards it. Enter this opening and follow the way as it wends upwards. Ahead of you the light is growing, as a soft turquoise-green glow, and as you approach it you begin to hear the sound of a waterfall. Now the mouth of the cave is before you, shrouded with green fronds. You push these aside and find yourself in a beautiful grotto, where glistens an emerald lake. Into the lake several crystal streams flow, over glistening rocks, entering the great body of water with a low chuckle. Droplets hang like pearls in the air. All is peace and freshness. Take a while to notice all the details of this beautiful place. [Pause.]

When you are ready, approach the lake and sit close to it, on a small rock. Now you notice that you are not alone, for graceful beings are coming close to you. These are the Undines or water spirits. Treat them with great respect and spend as much time with them as you and they wish, conversing or otherwise communicating. The Undines may have a message or a gift for you. This may be delivered in song, or in another way, or they may have things to show you. Receive what they offer with love and joy and pledge a gift in return. This may be connected to tending waterways, it may be a charitable gift to a cause, or connected to whales and dolphins. Leave with thanks and respect, when it feels right. Choose whether you wish to return to your sanctuary and the everyday, or whether you wish to continue.

If you wish to go on, follow the path around the lake, where it leads upwards and outwards, towards the early morning Sun. The path takes you higher and higher. Gradually you leave behind the trees and the shady places. The air is fresh and cool, and although you are climbing you feel exhilarated and clear-headed. Follow the path as it goes higher and higher. You are going up a mountain. [Pause.]

Now you are coming to the mountain top. You stand, as the wind plays around you, looking out over the vast panorama, the pattern of the fields, hedges, woodland and all the surrounding countryside. You can see from horizon to horizon. No longer deep within the Earth and the woodland, you are able to see where wood meets meadow, where the paths meander, where there is a crossroads or a bridge. All of the earth is laid out before you, and you feel a great sense of freedom, as the wind buffets you and the birds wheel and sing. [Pause.]

Now you become aware that there are beings around you, riding on the wind, swooping and wheeling. Hold out your arms to them, but do not try to hold them. These are the Sylphs, the spirits of the Air. They will have a gift or a message for you. Attend carefully to anything they may say, or show you. Pledge now a gift in return, anything that enhances your wisdom and powers of thought such as some study, writing or travel, or work for anything that helps the ozone layer or the atmosphere in general. Leave with thanks and respect only when it feels right for you and for the Sylphs. Choose now whether you wish to go on or return to your sanctuary and the everyday.

If you wish to go on, follow a path along the high ground, towards the midday Sun. How warm it is, and how energetic you are feeling, for this is a warmth that makes you glow and expand, feeling that all things are possible. Follow this path for a while. The air becomes sparkly and crackly, and fireworks are shooting skyward all around you, brightly visible in the noon sky. [Pause.]

Ahead of you, you notice that there is a great, golden temple. As you approach this you feel more and more energized, for the brightness seems to be penetrating through to your bones. As you enter the temple the Sun shines full through a round, gold and orange tinted window in the roof, forming a bright circle on the amber floor. The walls, the floor and the air itself are glowing and exuding energy. You dance around this circle, in joy. All seems possible. [Pause.]

Now you become aware that you are not alone in the temple. In the sunbeam and around the shining walls beings are dancing. These are the spirits of Fire, the Salamanders. Feel their vibrancy and partake of it. The salamanders will have a gift for you, or a message, or something to show you. Attend to this carefully, and pledge in return a creative act. Leave with thanks and respect only when it feels right to you and to the

> *Salamanders. Walk outside the temple, into the open air. State that you wish to return to your sanctuary.*
>
> *When in your sanctuary, pause for a while, to evaluate your experience. When you are ready, take off your travelling robe, and return to everyday awareness. Ground yourself and make a note of your experiences in your Book of Shadows. Always do what you have promised.*

Please note, if you choose to do this pathworking frequently you will need to make sure that the gifts you pledge are very small ones. The spirits of Nature do not demand sacrifice. What will help both you and them is contact, participation and understanding. The gifts you give will bring them into your life. Sometimes they may make suggestions and these may be very simple, such as lighting a candle, for Fire.

As you progress you will devise your own pathworking, or decide to follow a particular tradition that has its own models. Good journey!

SCRYING

Scrying is the art of looking for pictures within a 'speculum'. A speculum can be a crystal ball, a dark mirror or simply a bowl of water. Almost any surface that reflects will do, for all forms of mirrors are in a sense gateways to Otherworld. This is suggested by stories such as Lewis Carroll's *Through the Looking Glass* (1872), and folklore, such as the belief that vampires have no reflection. One of the meanings of this could be that vampires, having originated in Otherworld, are no longer to be found in the land beyond the mirror. Of course, science tells us that a mirror is a glass with a specific backing, which reflects light, and there is nothing behind our mirror but the wall. Younger Self, on the other hand, knows that a mirror is a door of perception

Scrying requires a state of very light trance that we may call 'magical consciousness'. It is a slightly drifty state that you will enter for rituals also. If you have perfected your relaxation and are able to open your chakras, do this and you will achieve the right state of mind. Let your mind drift as it does before going to sleep, but for this activity you will paradoxically be slightly 'entranced' and also sharply aware. You will need to empty your mind of distractions. Experimentation will discover what works best for you. Scrying is usually best undertaken by moonlight or candlelight.

Scrying is one of the arts of the witch. This is not just about 'foretelling the future' but about gaining insights. In a way it may be like an eyes-open pathworking. The images you see may seem to be literally before your eyes, or they may form in your 'mind's eye'. Do not be afraid of anything you see, for you may initially 'see' your fears and guilt. Scary images can also be merely symbols, for instance a skull does not usually mean a literal death at all, but probably a change. Scrying will open your inner sight and awareness.

The traditional time for scrying is at Samhain, when we may scry for meanings or messages about the coming year. If you are serious about scrying then it will be good to select your speculum with great care and cleanse and consecrate it in full ritual. Store your speculum away from common sight, with your magical things, and do not expose it to direct sunlight. Never let anyone else touch it, because then their 'energies' will inhabit your speculum and in all probability this will make you 'see' things that pertain to them – a process called psychometry. It is best to keep your speculum wrapped in a soft, black cloth.

If you choose to use a bowl of water for scrying, you may drop in it a silver coin or ring that you keep specially for this purpose, so that a point of light is reflected. You may prefer the surface to be dark. Whatever method you choose and whatever speculum you use, patience, practice and experiment are the key, until you find the conditions that work best for you. Please do not give up at the first attempt, because if you try again, eventually you will succeed. Do not 'talk yourself out' of anything that comes into your mind while you are gazing, for it may be important. Not everyone receives their experiences in the same way. Everything you receive is valuable, although some things are more valuable than others, of course. By valuing what you see and experience, these things will become clearer.

If, after you have been gazing for half an hour (and ten minutes might be best), you do not have a result, put the matter to one side and try again at another time, perhaps later in the night, at another Moon phase or whenever.

The purpose of scrying is to open your inner sight. If you become good at it you may use it to find answers to specific questions. Many witches are also fond of using tarot, runes, lithomancy (casting stones), astrology and other forms of the mantic arts. All of these are about developing your intuition, and even an astrological chart, for which there are precise rules in interpretation, may yield much more if looked at in the correct environment.

Pathwork Please embark on a routine of relaxation, progressing through the exercises, so that you are able to pathwork reasonably readily. When you are able to use your ability to pathwork in a way that enhances your life and your rituals, you will find it useful, enlightening and very beautiful.

Scrying Practise scrying or select one of the other magic arts of study and practice. Witches are not fortune-tellers, and by no means every witch has considerable psychic ability (in the same way that few psychics are witches). However, extending and deepening 'the sight' in order to access the wisdom of Otherworld is part of the path of the witch. Choose what suits you, and progress with it.

10

BECOMING A PRIESTESS OR PRIEST

It is not easy for us to change. But it is possible.
And it is our glory as human beings.

M. SCOTT PECK, *THE DIFFERENT DRUM* (1987)

EMBARKING ON THE PATH

If you have decided that the path of the witch is for you, then you are a witch. It needs no one else to confirm this, because it happens inside. However, witchcraft isn't merely a state: it is, as described, a path. All the time you will be developing, growing, changing, adapting and evolving. At one time in your life a particular form of the Craft may seem to be right for you, but at another things may look different. Do not be afraid to admit that you have changed, or that you wish to change direction. If you have been initiated into a tradition, this does not mean that you are imprisoned by it, and no true witch would ever wish to constrain or compel you in any way.

As a first step you may wish to initiate yourself. If this is the case you would be well advised to wait the traditional 'year and a day' before taking this step, taking the time to work through each of the sabbats, or work 13 times through the phases of the Moon. Deepen your wisdom with each cycle and study all that you can, not just in books (for a witch does not have to be an intellectual) but in inner exploration, pathworking, meditating and drawing close to Nature.

Experiencing and doing are essential. There isn't anything
to be gained by rushing things. The usual experience of
initiation is that it makes you more open, and you will need
to be prepared and strengthened for what may be
something of a psychic influx. Initiation does not mean that
you acquire the keys to a particular system, so much as that
you take on responsibility, make a commitment and open
yourself to experience.

CHOOSING YOUR COMPANIONS

Witchcraft groups are not cults. They do not tout for
members, evangelize, seduce and compel. Witches are
mostly fairly laidback people, who are, at the same time,
very ethical, possibly because they are so very aware of
having to live down all the bad press of the last two
millennia! Despite the fact that sexuality is celebrated and
rites may be conducted naked, witches' rites are not orgies.
Sex is rarely explicit or public and personal choice is always
paramount. Plenty of witches are involved in stable
relationships with all the usual fidelity and loyalty that is
valued in our culture.

Having said all of this, there are, of course, always the
exceptions, and unfortunately there will always be some
who seek to exploit the unwary, young and inexperienced,
to gratify their own egos or sexual desires. You need to be
aware of this, if you are contemplating joining a group.
Anyone who appears to be on an ego-trip or especially
lecherous is to be regarded with extreme caution. Go by
personal recommendation if you can, or consult the Pagan
Federation for recommended groups (see Resources). Do
not hesitate to leave if you feel the least uneasy, at any time
and do not allow yourself to be overawed, made to feel silly
naive or in any other way disempowered. If anyone tries to
take away your freedom or rob you of your power, by

manipulation, suggestion or whatever, they are not fit to lead you in any way, and if they purport to be 'superior' they are the opposite. Don't get caught in your inferiority complex – get out! A true teacher will always seek to empower you, and while there are always differences of personality and opinion, and we all have egos, you should always feel free to leave any situation that undermines you.

To find groups of like-minded people, look out for courses and activities advertised in your nearest New Age centre, shop or clinic. If you do not wish to join a formal grouping, but would simply like to meet others to celebrate festivals informally, or discuss and compare notes, you may find kindred spirits at such gatherings. One group may give you pointers to other venues, and if you are extravert, or feel you need the support of companions, you will need to do some searching. There are many choices, and it is impossible for me to describe all of them, partly because this will depend on what is available locally, but also because I certainly do not know about all the different approaches. Some indications have been given in this book about Wicca, and also about solitary working. However, within Wicca there are many variations in approach and content of rituals. Suggestions have also been included that are compatible with a Goddess approach. Some groups may be feminist Dianic witches, who only worship the Goddess, and with whom there may be a strong lesbian factor; other witches are traditional, coming from country customs or family heritage. Some witches claim to be hereditary, and it is true that some people come more naturally to the Craft, either because of experiences in earlier lifetimes or through gifts at birth. Some styles are more open and community orientated. If you feel the path of the solo witch is for you, that is fine, and there is nothing to stop you following the ways of the Mysteries in private.

When joining a group, especially an established one, things will need to 'feel right' both for you and for the long-standing members, because a newcomer may disrupt the flow of an experienced coven. If you are rejected, you are bound to feel bad at first, but do try not to take this too personally, because it isn't a comment on you, but upon your suitability for that particular group of people. It will turn out, in all probability, that they have done you a favour by turning you away, leaving you free to find something more suited to you. If you do join a group, remember witches can have a mischievous sense of humour, so don't take yourself too seriously! Another point is that rituals cost money and take time. Money is not usually charged for training in the Craft, but you will need to take your share of expenses in rituals, by bringing wine, candles, food for feasting etc. It is a nice touch to take care of your High Priest and Priestess, group leader or whoever, by bringing gifts sometimes, in acknowledgement of their hard work, time and provision of space. Remember also that the Craft will take up some prime time, for rituals are usually conducted at weekends, going late into Saturday night/Sunday morning, which can play havoc with other social commitments and also with partnerships, especially if your partner doesn't like or understand the Craft.

KEEPING RECORDS

In the old days everything was passed by word of mouth. People's memories were much better than they are now. Despite the fact that witchcraft is not intellectual, there is no substitute for keeping records, especially at first. It is all too easy to forget what you do and what happens in circle. If you do not plan your rituals you are likely to end up popping in and out of your circle for bits and pieces that you haven't thought to bring. While I am not of the opinion that you should never leave your circle once it is cast (you won't achieve much in a way of transcendency if you are dying for the loo, and as time seems to stand still in circle you may be there for quite a long time, drinking wine...) nonetheless, the circle should only be opened in necessity, and then carefully closed again. So write down your rituals in advance and make lists of what you need. Take your Book of Shadows into the circle with you, and write down anything important you experience, before closing down, or just after.

Place in your Book of Shadows anything that you plan, feel, meditate upon or have revelation about concerning the Craft. In addition to your Book of Shadows, keep a dream diary. In my opinion these two are essential. You may also like to have a Wheel of the Year workbook and a monthly menstrual mandala for female witches, or Moon diary. However, keep it simple. I think two books are enough. You don't want to spend all your time writing. And your notes don't have to be just writing. Stick in pictures, too, or draw them.

ETHICS

As a committed witch it is important that you are ethical, for you are a representative of the Craft. Ethics were discussed in Chapter 8. These boil down essentially to harming no one. Another factor to be born in mind is that all you do comes back to you. Never seek to influence another person or to interfere with their destiny. Healing spells may be another matter, although there are those who insist they should only be done by request. Here there are grey areas, and that is the essence of witchcraft, where you are thrown back on your own sense of responsibility and your own instincts, and you must live by your decisions. A further point is that you should not take money for spells. You should never obviously take money under false pretenses, because you can't ever be sure your spells will work for the person in the way they wish. I think we all get very uptight about money, which is, after all, essentially energy. There can be no harm in taking a gift from someone who can readily afford it. However, the question of doing spells for someone else is debatable, as we have seen.

An important point also is that no true witch leaves their witchcraft behind when they leave the circle. Witchcraft surely has to be about care for the environment, the natural world and for others. It is up to each witch to be as active politically as they wish, extending from tying oneself to threatened trees at the one end of the spectrum, to making political choices on the basis of pagan values. Not everyone is cut out to protest actively, but we each need to do what we feel able. Witchcraft isn't about reincarnated hair shirts, trying to shop for six people on a bike, or freezing in a cold house, because the Craft is about enjoying life. However, we should all try to live in awareness of our effect on the environment and do what we can within the constraints of our lifestyle. This may mean a bit of thought and organization, but it will mean that the whole of our life is an act of worship.

YOUNG PEOPLE AND THE CRAFT

Because witchcraft is an inner path and essentially a mystery tradition, most groups and covens will not consider initiating anyone under 18, and in some cases the minimum age is 21. Witches believe that everyone has the right to choose their own spiritual path, and that this decision cannot be made before maturity. It must also be said that witches are all too aware of their bad press as being sinister cults, child-abusers etc., and are going to the other extreme to prove this is not the case. While I certainly agree that we should all be free to make up our own minds several other factors also seem important. Firstly, some people are spiritually fairly mature before 18 (and some are not mature at 50!). Secondly, young people need guidance and information. My mail shows that an enormous number of young people (those under 16) are very interested in the Craft, paganism, and worship of Nature. Young people these days are more free to think and make up their own minds, and, to many, paganism and witchcraft seem logical! The Pagan Federation has begun to cater for these (in Minor Arcana, see Resources), but there is an enormous spiritual hunger as well as a great deal of emotional voltage in teenagers (hence the fact that poltergeists often centre around an adolescent). The most important point is that the young must not be exploited or indoctrinated, but I do feel they need more than just information and fellowship. They need to be able to develop their spirituality.

If you are young, my advice is to take things slowly, because however passionate and committed you now feel, you may change your mind. Even if it comes naturally to you, it will still take time to learn the Craft. Working through the Wheel of the Year will take at least one year, in any case, and will help to ground you. Also, witchcraft is mind-expanding and mind-altering, and this can be stressful to anyone and especially so to a young mind. This is not to say 'don't' because this is safer then taking recreational drugs or driving too fast, too often. However, always be sure you use the proper safeguards, about grounding and closing down your circle, and keep your life in balance. This means you should not let the Craft take over from daily activities, such as studies, friends, sports and similar. Sadly, I also have to say do be careful about any older people who offer to lead you, because it is possible their motives are not pure (it is also possible they are pure, of course).

If you are an older person with experience of witchcraft, and you are being asked for information and even training by someone young, remember, that if you are too cagey in your wish not to influence them you will invest the Craft with lots of glamour and mystery and you will influence them that way! My advice is to give all the information you can, in a way that can be understood. If the young person wants to take part in rituals, it is quite possible for these to be informal and undemanding. It is usually possible, with common sense, to see just how much someone can take, and again, providing there is a reasonable balance of other interests, things should evolve in their own time, resulting hopefully, in time, in a powerful and wise personality, deeply experienced in the Craft. As witchcraft and paganism grow in popularity, these are matters that will no doubt be more fully addressed in the new millennium.

THE IMPORTANCE OF THE GOD

For most witches the Goddess comes first. This really means first in order of remembering, not in a hierarchy. However, there is something very important about exalting the Feminine, and this really is twofold. In rediscovering the Goddess we return to our roots, develop our instincts and our sense of the Earth upon which we tread as an object of worship. We re-soul the material world. We also enable the Feminine to regain strength, and this means that individual women can find their true strength within, not by reference to patriarchal values. In so doing masculine values are not denigrated, or the emergence of ego-consciousness and the use of logic regarded as bad. Rather the balance is beginning to be redressed, for we can hopefully find our way back to 'the Garden' in knowledge of what it is and what it means, so blending the mystical and the rational, with a view to a quantum leap into a new state. In addition by giving due reverence and power to the Feminine, the Masculine can grow and flourish in a new maturity. Witchcraft, in its Goddess worship, offers a means of growth to women and men. By encouraging power, independence and also intense femininity in women, the way is paved for men who also wish to grow also, and to find new depth and meaning in their masculinity, when they also are freed from patriarchal stereotypes.

INITIATION

If you have decided that you wish to join a group such as a Wiccan coven, they will no doubt have their own styles and requirements, and you will need to find out about these. Being initiated into one tradition does not preclude being initiated into another, and self-initiation can precede initiation by others, or not. To initiate yourself you need only to feel ready, but please remember that initiation will leave you more open. Rather than offering you some sort of spiritual protection, the experience is usually that you have more to deal with, psychically and sometimes in the external world. You are making a powerful commitment that resonates through all levels of the Soul, and the result could be anything from feeling 'spaced out' through to being flooded with memories of a previous incarnation, and having your inner eye opened and bombarded with many images. So this isn't something to be taken lightly. Approach your decision by meditation and pathworking. I have suggested a year and a day as a good run-up period, but in the end the decision is yours. Here is a simple ritual to initiate yourself as a witch and a follower of the Goddess.

If you feel ready to initiate yourself, give yourself one Moon (one passage of the Moon from New Moon back to New again) and time your initiation for three or four days after New Moon, when the first sickle is visible in the evening sky. Meditate on each of the days during your lead-up time, take walks and spend some time in seclusion. Reflect on and learn about anything that feels appropriate, such as goddesses and gods from different mythologies, tree lore, shamanism or similar subjects.

It is usual to choose a 'witch name' to affirm your new, inner identity as witch and priestess or priest. This may be chosen from mythological names of goddesses, gods and heroes, or may be something from the natural world, such as Rowan, Willow or similar. Choose your name and then give yourself one night to dream about it. Even if you do not remember any dream, you should wake up feeling good about your choice, or that it is inappropriate.

When the time approaches that you have chosen for your initiation, you will need to make arrangements so that you can be alone. Ideally, you should spend the 24 hours before on your own. Sleep alone, and take a walk in the country, if possible. Come back and purify yourself by taking a bath with salt or lavender oil. For the ceremony you will need an old shirt or robe, which you are prepared to shred and burn, and some initiation oil, made from oils of frankincense, myrrh and sandalwood, dissolved in a carrier oil such as grapeseed, (two drops of essential oil to one teaspoon of carrier). You will also need some wine, some cake and some scissors, in addition to the usual ritual accoutrements. For your incense choose a combination of frankincense, benzoin, sandalwood, bay and a pinch of dragon's blood, or choose the Fire of Azrael incense, sandalwood, cedar and juniper. (Failing these, many blends will do, and a proprietary Imbolc blend, for instance, should be very suitable.)

Begin your ritual after sundown. Wear your old shirt or robe, and have a fresh one handy, if you wish. Cast your circle and begin to burn incense. Allow a peaceful, dreamy feeling to steal over you. Take your time. Sit in the centre of your circle, watching the coils of incense smoke rising. Meditate and draw closer to the Goddess.

When you feel ready, face North and curl yourself up in a foetal position. Then slowly rise to a standing position. Pull off your old robe. Hold your arms upwards, and offer yourself to the powers of Earth, in whatever words seem appropriate, asking for their protection and help and pledging your allegiance to the subtle realms. You might say, for instance:

> *O Powers of Earth, Nature spirits, Gnomes and devas, I pledge myself as guardian of the Earth and respecter of all that lives, and I ask that you give me your protection, grounding, health, good sense and balance.*

Turn now to East with similar words:

> *O Powers of Air, Sylphs and aerial spirits, give me clear thought, freedom and inspiration. I pledge myself as guardian of the pure air.*

Now turn to the South, with words such as:

> *O Powers of Fire, Salamanders, give me passion, energy, imagination and creativity. I pledge myself as guardian of the inner fires of the spirit.*

And finally turn to the West, saying:

> *O Powers of Water, Undines and spirits of lake, sea and river, give me compassion, love and wisdom. I pledge myself as guardian of the waters and a vessel of love.*

Turn now back to the East, saying something like:

> *Bright Goddess, lady of the awakened soul, accept me… [name] as witch and priestess [priest]. In full knowledge of my choice I set my feet upon your path and dedicate myself in your ancient names. Isis, Aradia, Bridget, Diana. Great Horned One, God of the witches, protect me, help and guide me. Fill me with joy and energy. Lugh, Cernunnos, Hermes, Thoth.*

Here you will naturally wish to choose your own names and style of invocation. Dedicate your oil by passing it over the candle flame, through the incense smoke, over your chalice or cauldron, and set it upon your pentacle or stone. Now trace an invoking pentagram over it, with your finger or athame. Anoint yourself between the eyes, on the chest, and the genitals, with the words:

> *May the mind be free. May the heart be free. May the body be free.*

Light more incense and stand in the centre if your circle, facing North (or South, in the southern hemisphere). Reflect for a while. Then say:

> *Old Ones, Goddess and God, Powers of the Cosmos, I stand before you as witch and priestess [priest].*

Sit now, for as long as you wish, gazing into the incense smoke, or into your cauldron. Feel yourself expand, mingling with the powers of life. Feel them accepting you, in joy, peace and love. Notice all the images that come to your mind. In the cauldron of your circle you are now being reborn as representative of the Goddess. You may want to put on your new robe at this point.

When you feel ready, stand up, with arms raised and walk or dance around your circle, in joy. If you feel peaceful, tired or a little drained, just take it easy. Announce, 'My new life in the Goddess and the God begins here.' Consecrate wine and cake, and eat and drink in celebration. Shred your old robe, and burn it later, if you can.

Make a final toast, and close down your circle, when you are ready. Be especially thorough on this occasion. Take special note of your dreams on the night that follows.

Feel free to alter the ritual if you wish in ways that seem appropriate. And may you be blessed on your path.

FURTHER READING AND RESOURCES

Relevant books by the same author:

Witchcraft: A Beginner's Guide; Shamanism: A Beginner's Guide; Paganism: A Beginner's Guide; The Goddess: A Beginner's Guide; Herbs for Magic and Ritual: A Beginner's Guide; Spells and Rituals: A Beginner's Guide; The Magic and Mystery of Trees: A Beginner's Guide; Earth Mysteries: A Beginner's Guide; Pagan Gods (with Howard Moorey); *The Wheel of the Year: Myth and Magic Through the Seasons* (with Jane Brideson). All published by Hodder & Stoughton

Other works

Adler, Margot, *Drawing Down the Moon* (Beacon, 1986)

Baring, Anne, and Cashford, Jules, *The Myth of the Goddess: Evolution of an Image* (Arkana, 1993)

Beth, Rae, *Hedge Witch* (Hale, 1990)

Brennan, J.H., *Experimental Magic* (Aquarian, 1972)

Crowley, Vivianne, *Wicca: The Old Religion in the New Age* (Aquarian, 1989)

Cunningham, Scott, *Crystal, Gem and Metal Magic* (Llewellyn, 1994), *The Complete Book of Incense, Oils and Brews* (Llewellyn, 1991)

Farrar, Janet and Stewart, *Eight Sabbats for Witches* (Hale, 1989) *Spells and How they Work* (Hale, 1990), *The Witches' Goddess* (Phoenix, 1987), *The Witches' God* (Phoenix, 1989)

Fortune, Dion, *The Mystical Qabalah* (Aquarian, 1987)

Gimbutas, Marija, *The Language of the Goddess* (Thames & Hudson, 1989)

Gooch, Stan, *Cities of Dreams: When Women Ruled the Earth* (Aulis, 1995)

Graves, Robert, *The White Goddess* (Faber & Faber, 1988)

Green, Marian, *A Witch Alone* (Aquarian, 1991), *A Calendar of Festivals* (Element, 1991)

Johnson, Buffie, *Lady of the Beasts* (Traditions International, 1994)

Jones, Kathy, *The Ancient British Goddess* (Ariadne, 1991)

Lantiere, Joe, *Witchcraft's History Outlined*

Leland, Charles, *Aradia* or *Gospel of the Witches* (Phoenix, 1990)

Matthews, Caitlin (ed.), *Voices of the Goddess* (Aquarius, 1990)

McCrickard, Janet, *Eclipse of the Sun* (Element, 1995)

Monaghan, Patricia, *The Book of Goddesses and Heroines* (Llewellyn, 1989)

Murray, Margaret, *The Witch Cult in Western Europe* (Oxford, 1921), *The God of the Witches* (Daimon, 1962), *The Divine King in England* (Faber & Faber, 1954)

Ozaniec, Naomi, *Chakras for Beginners* (Hodder & Stoughton, 1994)

Ransom, Victoria, and Bernstein, Henriette, *The Crone Oracles* (Weiser, 1994)

Ryall, Rhiannon, *West Country Wicca* (Capall Bann, 1993)

Sams, Jamie, *13 Original Clan Mothers* (HarperCollins, 1994)

Shan, *Circlework* (House of the Goddess, 1994)

Sheldrake, Rupert, *A New Science of Life* (Flamingo, 1995)

Shuttle, Penelope, and Redgrove, Peter, *The Wise Wound* (HarperCollins, 1994)

Starhawk, *The Spiral Dance* (Harper & Row, 1979)

Valiente, Doreen, *An ABC of Witchcraft: Past & Present* (Hale, 1973), *Witchcraft for Tomorrow* (Hale, 1993)

Wilson, Colin, *From Atlantis to the Sphinx* (Virgin, 1997)